Albert Gallatin Mackey

The Book of the Chapter

Or, Monitorial Instructions, in the degrees of mark, past and most excellent Master,

and the holy Royal Arch. Fourth Edition

Albert Gallatin Mackey

The Book of the Chapter
Or, Monitorial Instructions, in the degrees of mark, past and most excellent Master, and the holy Royal Arch. Fourth Edition

ISBN/EAN: 9783337078003

Printed in Europe, USA, Canada, Australia, Japan

Cover: Foto ©ninafisch / pixelio.de

More available books at **www.hansebooks.com**

THE

BOOK OF THE CHAPTER:

OR

MONITORIAL INSTRUCTIONS,

IN THE DEGREES OF

MARK, PAST AND MOST EXCELLENT MASTER,

AND THE

Holy Royal Arch.

BY ALBERT G. MACKEY, M. D.,

GRAND HIGH PRIEST OF THE GRAND ROYAL ARCH CHAPTER OF SOUTH CAROLINA; AUTHOR OF
A "LEXICON OF FREEMASONRY," "PRINCIPLES OF MASONIC LAW," ETC.

———————

"These mysteries are so profound and so exalted, that they can be compre-
hended by those only who are enlightened."—CYRIL OF ALEXANDRIA.

———————

FOURTH EDITION.

NEW YORK:

MACOY & SICKELS, PUBLISHERS, 430 BROOME STREET.

1863.

TO

HON. CHARLES SCOTT,

PAST GRAND MASTER AND PAST GRAND HIGH PRIEST OF MISSISSIPPI,

THIS WORK

Is Dedicated

AS A

SLIGHT TOKEN OF THE SINCERE FRIENDSHIP

OF THE

AUTHOR.

CONTENTS.

PREFACE.

IT must be acknowledged that there is no dearth of ordinary monitorial books, although I know of none exclusively appropriated to the Chapter degrees. But an experience, by no means inconsiderable, has forced upon me the conviction that the plan upon which these works have been hitherto constructed, is not such as to meet the demands of the enlarged masonic intellect of the present day. All the Monitors now extant appear to have adopted that of THOMAS SMITH WEBB as their prototype, and, like it, have been very generally confined to the arrangement of the prayers, charges, and Scripture lessons, which are used in the several degrees, without any, or, at most, a very slight attempt to explain, by commentaries, the symbolic meaning or the historical references of the different portions of the ritual. Hence, but very little knowledge, beyond the mere working part of our institution, is to be obtained from these books; and although they are well enough for that purpose, still, as it is not the only purpose which may and ought to be effected by a Monitor, I have sought to present the masonic reader with something more in the ensuing pages.

Many masons, although willing, and, indeed, anxious, as

soon as they are initiated, to learn something more of the
nature of the institution into which they have been introduced, and of the meaning of the ceremonies through
which they have passed, are very often unable, from the
want of times or means, to indulge this laudable curiosity.
The information which they require is to be found only in
the pages of various masonic treatises, and to be acquired
only by careful and laborious study.   Books are not
always accessible, or if accessible, leisure or inclination
may be wanting to institute the necessary investigations.

But a Monitor is within every mason's reach.   It is the
first book to which his attention is directed, and is often
placed in his hands by the presiding officer, as a manual
which he is recommended to study; and, accordingly, the
Monitor is to many a mason, emphatically, his *vade mecum*.
But unless he can find something more important in its
pages than such works as those of WEBB and CROSS contain, he will scarcely arise from the perusal with any in-
creased store of knowledge. His want is for " more light "
—not for a recapitulation of what he has already heard
and seen, but for a rational explanation of the meaning of
that through which he has passed.

To meet this want, and to place in the hands of every
Royal Arch Mason a book in which he may find a lucid
explanation, so far as the laws of our institution will permit, of all that has excited his curiosity or attracted his
interest in the Chapter degrees, and above all, to furnish
an elementary treatise of easy comprehension on the symbolism of Royal Arch Masonry, have been the objects of
the author in the preparation of the present work. The

plan upon which it has been written is a novel and hitherto untried one. Yet he thinks that he knows enough, from past experience of the wants of young as well as of old masons, to authorize him to anticipate, with some confidence, its favorable acceptance by the craft. His design, at all events, has been a meritorious one; and if there be any defects or imperfections in the execution, he has, at least, intended, by this labor, to elevate the standard and increase the usefulness of monitorial instruction.

ALBERT G. MACKEY, M. D.

CHARLESTON, May 1st, 1858.

BOOK I.

Mark Master.

"By the influence of Mark Master Degree, the work of every operative mason was distinctly known. The perfect stones were received with acclamations; while those that were deficient were rejected with disdain. The arrangement proved a superior stimulus to exertion, which accounts for the high finish which the temple subsequently acquired."

OLIVER'S HISTORICAL LANDMARKS.

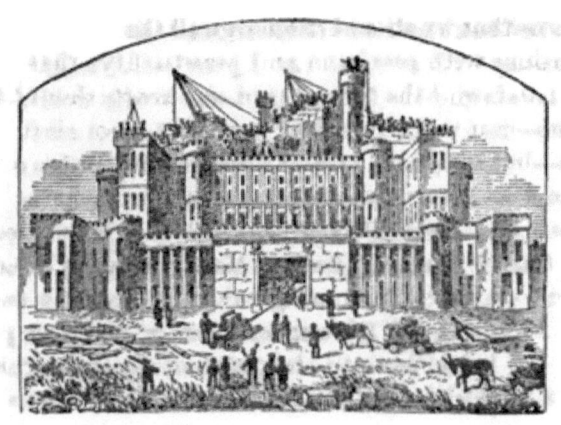

FOURTH DEGREE.

SYMBOLICAL DESIGN.

The degree of Mark Master, which is the fourth in the masonic series, is, historically considered, of the utmost importance, since we are informed that, by its influence, each operative mason, at the building of King Solomon's temple, was known and distinguished, and the disorder and confusion, which might otherwise have attended so immense an undertaking, was completely prevented, and not only the craftsmen themselves, but every part of their workmanship was discriminated with the greatest nicety and the utmost facility. If defects were found, the overseers, by the help of this degree, were enabled, without difficulty, to ascertain who was the faulty workman; so that all deficiencies might be remedied, without injuring the credit or diminishing the reward of the industrious and faithful among the craft.*

Not less useful is it in its symbolic signification. As illustrative of the Fellow Craft's degree, it is particularly directed to the inculcation of order, regularity, and discipline. It

* Webb's Monitor, p. 84, edit. 1808.

teaches us that we should discharge all the duties of our several stations with precision and punctuality; that the work of our hands and the thoughts of our hearts should be good and true—not unfinished and imperfect—not sinful and defective—but such as the Great Overseer and Judge of heaven and earth will see fit to approve as a worthy oblation from his creatures. If the Fellow Craft's degree is devoted to the inculcation of learning, that of Mark Master is intended to instruct us how that learning can most usefully and judiciously be employed for our own honor and the profit of others. It holds forth to the desponding the encouraging thought, that although our motives may sometimes be misinterpreted by our erring fellow-mortals, our attainments be underrated, and our reputations be traduced by the envious and malicious, there is One, at least, who sees not with the eyes of man, but may yet make that stone which the builders rejected the head of the corner. The intimate connection, then, between the second and fourth degrees of Masonry is this, that while one inculcates the necessary exercise of all the duties of life, the other teaches the importance of performing them with systematic regularity. The true Mark Master is a type of that man, mentioned in the sacred parable, who received from his Master this approving language: " Well done, good and faithful servant; thou hast been faithful over a few things, I will make thee ruler over many things: enter thou into the joys of thy Lord."

HISTORICAL SUMMARY.

We learn, from the traditions of Freemasonry, that the order of Mark Masters, at the temple of Solomon, was selected from the great body of the Fellow Crafts.

According to these traditions, there were two divisions of the Fellow Crafts. The first, or higher class, worked in the quarries, in finishing the stones, or, as we may say, in our lectures, "in hewing, squaring, and numbering" them; and that each one might be enabled to designate his own work, he was in possession of a mark which he placed upon the stones prepared by him. Hence, this class of Fellow Crafts were called **Mark Masters**, and received their pay from the Senior **Grand Warden**, whom some suppose to have been Adoniram, the brother-in-law of Hiram Abif, and the first of the Provosts and Judges. These Fellow Crafts received their pay in money, at the rate of a half shekel of silver per day, equal to about twenty-five cents. They were paid weekly, at the sixth hour of the sixth day of the week, that is to say, on Friday, at noon. And this hour appears to have been chosen, because, as we are taught in the third degree, at noon, or high twelve, the Craft were always called from labor to refreshment, and hence the payment of their wages at that hour would not interfere with, or retard the progress of, the work. And Friday was selected as the day, because the following one was the Sabbath, or day of rest, when all labor was suspended.

But the other and larger division of the Fellow Crafts, being younger and more inexperienced men, and with less skill and knowledge, were not advanced to the grade of **Mark Masters**. These were not, therefore, in possession of a mark. They proved their claim to reward by another token, and, after that part of the edifice was completed, received their wages in the middle chamber of the temple, being paid in corn, wine, and oil, agreeably to the stipulation of King Solomon with Hiram of Tyre.

OPENING OF THE LODGE.

A LODGE of Mark Masters consists, besides the Tiler, of the following eleven officers:

RIGHT WORSHIPFUL MASTER.

SENIOR WARDEN.*

JUNIOR WARDEN.

TREASURER.

SECRETARY.

SENIOR DEACON.

JUNIOR DEACON.

MASTER OVERSEER.

SENIOR OVERSEER.

JUNIOR OVERSEER.

MASTER OF CEREMONIES.

These offices are filled by the officers of the Chapter under whose warrant the Mark Lodge is held, in the following order:

The High Priest, King, and Scribe, act as Master and Wardens; the Treasurer and Secretary occupy the corresponding stations; the Principal Sojourner acts as Senior Deacon; the Royal Arch Captain, as Junior Deacon; the Grand Master of the Third Veil, as Master Overseer; the Grand Master of the Second Veil, as Senior Overseer; the Grand Master of the First Veil, as Junior Overseer; and the Captain of the Host, as Master of Ceremonies.

* In the ritual of reception this officer is styled "Senior Grand Warden."

The symbolic color of the Mark degree is purple.* The apron is of white lamb-skin, edged with purple, and the collar of purple, edged with gold. But as Mark lodges are no longer independent bodies, but always held under the warrant of a Royal Arch Chapter, the collars, aprons and jewels of the Chapter are generally made use of in conferring the Mark degree.

Lodges of Mark Masters are "dedicated to Hiram, the Builder." A candidate receiving this degree is said to be "advanced to the honorary degree of a Mark Master."

CHARGE

TO BE READ AT OPENING THE LODGE.

Wherefore, brethren, lay aside all malice, and guile, and hypocrisies, and envies, and all evil speakings.

If so be ye have tasted that the Lord is gracious, to whom coming as unto a living stone, disallowed indeed of men, but chosen of God, and precious; ye also as living stones, be ye built up a spiritual house, an holy priesthood, to offer up sacrifices acceptable to God.

Wherefore, also, it is contained in the scripture, Behold, I lay in Zion, for a foundation, a tried stone, a precious corner-stone, a sure foundation; he that believeth, shall not make haste to pass it over. Unto you, therefore, which believe, it is an honor; and even to them which be disobedient, the stone

---

* Yellow was formerly appropriated to this degree, and was used in Mark lodges working under the Ancient and Accepted Rite.

which the builders disallowed, the same is made the head of the corner.

Brethren, this is the will of God, that with well-doing ye put to silence the ignorance of foolish men. As free, and not using your liberty for a cloak of maliciousness, but as the servants of God. Honor all men ; love the brotherhood ; fear God.

The passages of Scripture here selected are peculiarly appropriate to this degree. The repeated references to the "living stone," to the "tried stone," the "precious corner-stone," and more especially to "the stone which the builders disallowed," are intended to impress the mind not only with the essential ceremonies of the degree, but also with its most important and significant symbol. The passages are taken, with slight but necessary modifications, from the 2d chapter of the First Epistle of Peter and the 28th chapter of Isaiah.

LECTURE AND RITUAL.

THE lecture on the fourth degree of Masonry is divided into two sections, each of which is appropriately exemplified by a corresponding section of the ritual of initiation.

First Section.

The first section exemplifies the regularity and good order that were observed by the craftsmen at the building of the temple, illustrates the method by which the idle and unworthy were detected and punished, and displays the legend which recounts one of the principal events which characterizes this degree.

The attention of the neophyte is particularly directed, in the ceremonies of this section, to the materials of which the temple was constructed, the place whence they were obtained, and the method in which they were inspected and approved, or rejected.

Workmen from the Quarries.

The materials of which the temple of King Solomon was principally constructed consisted of the compact mountain limestone which is almost the entire geological formation of Palestine, and which rises above the surface in the rocky hillocks on which the city of Jerusalem is built.

This stone is very solid, of a nearly white color, and capable of receiving a remarkable polish.*

Ancient quarries of this rock still abound in the Holy Land, and, although long since disused, present the internal evidence of having been employed for purposes of building. One of them, beneath the city of Jerusalem, and undoubtedly the very quarry from which Solomon obtained most of his material, has been but lately discovered. Mr. PRIME, who visited this quarry in 1856, speaks of it thus:

"That the whole was a quarry was amply evident. The unfinished stone, the marks of places whence many had been taken, the galleries, in the ends of which were marked out the blocks to be cut, and the vast masses cut, but never removed, all showed sufficiently the effect of the cutting. But date or inscription we looked in vain for, and conjecture is left free here. I wandered hour after hour through the vast halls, seeking some evidence of their origin.

* A writer in the "Boston Traveller," who visited the quarries beneath Jerusalem, describes the stones as being "extremely soft and pliable, nearly white, and very easily worked, but, like the stones of Malta and Paris, hardening by exposure."

One thing to me is very manifest. There has been solid stone taken from this excavation sufficient to build the walls of Jerusalem and the Temple of Solomon. The size of many of the stones taken from here appears to be very great. I know of no place to which the stone can have been carried but to these works, and I know of no other quarries in the neighborhood from which the great stone of the walls would seem to have come. These two connected ideas impelled me strongly towards the belief that this was the ancient quarry whence the city was built, and when the magnitude of the excavation between the two opposing hills and of this cavern is considered, it is, to say the least of it, a difficult question to answer, what has become of the stone once here, on any other theory than that I have suggested."*

This quarry has received, in modern days, the name of the " Cave of Jeremiah." It is situated on the Hill of Acra, west of the temple.

Another modern traveler says: "I have roamed abroad over the surrounding hills, even to Mizpeh, where Samuel testified, and into the long, deep limestone quarries beneath Jerusalem itself, whence Solomon obtained those splendid slabs, the origin of which has been so long unknown. It is but four years since the existence of this immense subterranean cavern was known to travelers. I have penetrated it for near half a mile, and seen there many large stones already cut, which were prepared for work, but were never removed. This new discovery is one of the greatest wonders of Jerusalem. It seems to extend under the temple itself, and the stones were all finished and dressed there, and then raised up at the very spot for their appropriation."†

It is evident, therefore, that the quarries whence the Mark Masters obtained their materials were situated in the immediate vicinity of the temple.

---

* Tent Life in the Holy Land, p. 113.
† Christian Witness, Sept. 11, 1857.

Stones of a finer quality were also obtained from the mountains of Lebanon, and were prepared by the workmen of Hiram, King of Tyre.

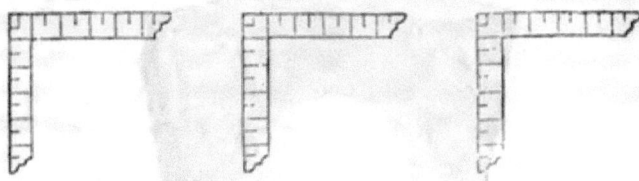

Good work—True work—Square work.

The work of all the *materials brought up for the building of the temple* was required to be good, true, and square, and such only, our traditions inform us, were the overseers authorized to receive.

Good work—made of the best materials, not defective, but accurately and neatly finished, and thus fit and suitable, by its workmanlike appearance, for a place in the magnificent building for which it was intended.

True work—right to precision in all its dimensions and surfaces, neither too long nor too short, too thick nor too thin, but level on its top and bottom, and perpendicular on its sides, so as to be exactly conformable to the copy or pattern which had been inscribed by the master builder on his trestle-board.

Square work—that the joints of the stones might be accurately adapted, and each part fitted with such exact nicety that the whole, when completed, might seem to be "rather the workmanship of the Supreme Architect than of mere human hands."

And all this is in conformity not only with the traditions of Masonry, but with the teachings of the Scriptures, which inform us that "the house, when it was in building, was built of stone made ready before it was brought thither : so that there was neither hammer nor axe, nor any tool of iron, heard in the house while it was in building."*

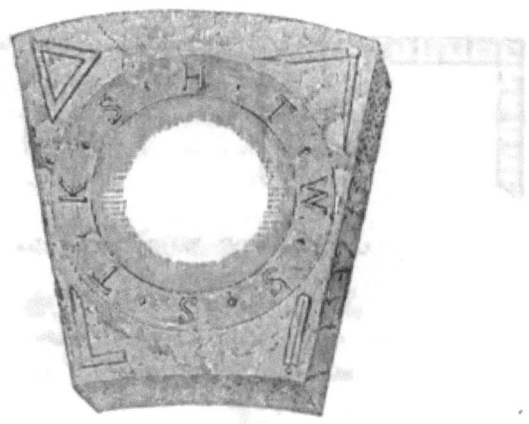

The regular Mark of the Craft.

OLIVER says that, at the building of the temple, certain men were employed to mark the materials as they came out of the hands of the workmen, that no false mark might be placed upon an imperfect stone, and to enable them to be put together with greater facility and precision, when conveyed from the quarries to the holy mountain of Moriah. This is not exactly the tradition. Each workman placed his own mark upon his own materials, so that the workmanship of every mason might be readily distinguished, and praise or blame be justly awarded. These marks, according to the lectures, consisted of mathematical figures, squares, angles, lines, and perpendiculars, and hence any figure of a different kind would not be deemed "the regular mark of the craft." A similar custom was practised by the masons of the middle

---

* I. Kings, vi. 7. The writer in the "Boston Traveller," quoted, says, when speaking of the quarry beneath Jerusalem, " the heaps of chippings which lie about show that the stone was dressed *on the spot*, which accords with the account of the building of the temple."

ages, and many of the stones, both inside and outside of the cathedrals and other buildings of that period were thus marked. Mr. GODWIN, in a communication to the Society of Antiquaries, says, that "in his opinion, these marks, if collected and compared, might assist in connecting the various bands of operatives, who, under the protection of the Church—mystically united—spread themselves over Europe during the middle ages, and are known as Freemasons."

The sixth hour of the sixth day of the week.

The Jews divided the day into twelve hours, commencing at sun-rise and ending at sun-set. The hours, therefore, varied in length with the variations of the seasons. Mid-day was, however, always the sixth hour, and sun-set the twelfth. At the equinoxes, for instance, when the sun rose at six o'clock, the hours of the day were apportioned as follows: Seven o'clock was the first hour; eight, the second; nine, the third; ten, the fourth; eleven, the fifth; and twelve, the sixth. The sixth hour, or "high twelve," was appropriately selected as the time of paying the craft their wages, because, being then called from labor to refreshment, the progress of the work was not impeded by the interruption of paying the workmen, which would have been the case at any other time.

The week commencing on Sunday, and ending on Saturday, or the Sabbath, the sixth day was accordingly Friday, and hence 12 o'clock, noon, on Friday, is the time designated by "**the sixth hour of the sixth day of the week.**" **The labors of** the week **were** then **concluded, and the rest** of the time, **to** sunset or the twelfth hour, **was probably occupied** in paying off the workmen.

An important lesson is here allegorically taught, which may be communicated in the sublime language of Brother ALBERT PIKE:

"Be careful, my brother, that thou receive no wages, here or elsewhere, that are not thy due. For if thou dost, thou wrongest some one, by taking that which **in** God's chancery **belongs to** Him;—and whether that which thou takest **thus, be** **wealth, or** rank, or influence, or reputation."

Second Section.

In this section the Mark Master is instructed in the origin and history of the degree. By a symbolical lesson, of impressive character, he is taught the duty of aiding a distressed brother. A variety of interesting circumstances connected with the building of King Solomon's temple are detailed, and the marks of distinction which were in use among our ancient brethren are explained.

The Symbolic allusion of the *Indenting Chisel* and the *Mallet* is one of the first things to which the attention of the candidate is directed.

 The Chisel and Mallet are used by operative masons to hew, cut, carve,  and indent their work ; but, as Mark Masters, we are taught to employ them for a more noble and glorious purpose ; they teach us to hew, cut, carve and indent the principles of morality and virtue on our minds.

The following passages of Scripture are here appropriately introduced.

The stone which the builders refused is become the head stone of the corner.—*Ps.* cxviii. 22.

Did ye never read in the Scriptures, the stone which the builders rejected is become the head of the corner ?—*Matt.* xxi. 42.

And have you not read this Scripture, the stone which the builders rejected is become the head of the corner ?—*Mark* xii. 10.

What is this, then, that is written, the stone which the builders rejected is become the head of the corner ?—*Luke* xx. 17.

The MARK, whose peculiar use should be here practically exemplified, is the appropriate jewel of a Mark Master. It is made of gold or silver, usually of the former metal, and must be in the form of a keystone. On the obverse or front surface the device or "mark" selected by the owner must be engraved, within a circle composed of the following letters : H. T. W. S. S. T. K. S. On the reverse or posterior surface, the name of the owner, the name of his chapter, and the date of his advancement, may be inscribed, although this is not absolutely necessary. The "mark" consists of the device and surrounding inscription on the obverse.

It is not requisite that the device or mark should be of a strictly masonic character, although masonic emblems are frequently selected in preference to other subjects. As soon as adopted it should be drawn or described in a book kept by the chapter for that purpose, and it is then said to be "recorded in the Book of Marks," after which time it can never be changed by the possessor for any other, or altered in the slightest degree, but remains as his "mark" to the day of his death.

This mark is not a mere ornamental appendage of the degree, but is a sacred token of the rites of friendship and brotherly love, and its presentation at any time by the owner to another Mark Master, would claim, from the latter, certain acts of friendship, which are of solemn obligation among the fraternity. A mark thus presented, for the purpose of obtaining a favor, is said to be *pledged ;* though remaining in the possession of the owner, it ceases, for any actual purposes of advantage, to be his property ; nor can it be again used by him, until, either by the return of the favor, or the consent of the benefactor, it has been redeemed ; for it is a positive law of the order, that no Mark Master shall " pledge his mark a second time until he has redeemed it from its previous pledge." By this wise provision, the unworthy are prevented from making an improper use of this valuable token, or from levying contributions on their hospitable brethren.

The use of a similar token was of great antiquity among the Greeks and Romans. With the former people, when a host had entertained a stranger, who was about to depart, he broke a die in two, one half of which he himself retained, while the other half was presented to the guest, so that if, at any future period, they, or any of their descendants, should meet again, a means of recognition was established, and the hospitable connection was renewed, or its favors returned. Among the Romans a similar custom prevailed, and the mark or die was called *tessera hospitalis,* or " the hospitable token." It descended from father to son, and the claim of friendly assistance that it had established could only be abolished by a formal renunciation, and the breaking of the tessera to pieces.*

The primitive Christians used a similar token, on which the initials of the Greek words for Father, Son, and Holy Ghost were inscribed. It served in the place of a certificate of Christian membership, and, being carried by them from town to town, secured the assistance and protection of their brethren.

---

* See an interesting Masonic tale, entitled " The Broken Tessera," in *Lights and Shadows of Freemasonry,* by Rob Morris, p. 289.

JEWISH SHEKEL.

The value of a mark is said to be "a Jewish half shekel of silver, or twenty-five cents in the currency of this country." The shekel of silver was a weight of great antiquity among the Jews, its value being about a half dollar. It is more than probable that there was a coin of fixed value in the days of Solomon, but the earliest specimens which have reached the present times, and are to be found in the cabinets of collectors, are of the coinage of Simon Maccabeus, issued about the year 144 B. C. Of these, we generally find, on the obverse, the sacred pot of manna, with the inscription, "Shekel Israel," in the old Samaritan character; on the reverse, the rod of Aaron, having three buds, with the inscription, "Ierushalem Kadoshah," or Jerusalem the Holy, in a similar character.

We learn from the Book of Exodus that every Israelite above twenty years of age was compelled to pay an annual poll-tax of half a shekel, as a contribution to the sanctuary, which was hence called "the offering of the Lord." The consecration of the Jewish half shekel of silver to so holy a purpose as the support of the sanctuary and the temple, is undoubtedly the reason why it has been adopted in Masonry as the value of the Mark.

Certain passages of Scripture are here referred to as explanatory of the subsequent investiture with important secrets of the degree.

II. CHRONICLES, ii. 16.

And we will cut wood out of Lebanon, as much as thou shalt need ; and we will bring it to thee in floats by sea, to Joppa, and thou shalt carry it up to Jerusalem.

A circumstance of great interest in the account of Joppa, so far as relates to this degree, is its difficulty as a port of entrance. JOSEPHUS, in describing it, says : "Joppa is not naturally a haven, for it ends in a rough shore, where all the rest of it is strait, but the two ends bend towards each other, where there are deep precipices and great stones, that jet out into the sea, and where the chains wherewith Andromeda was bound have left their impressions, which attest the antiquity of that fable. But the north wind opposes and beats upon the shore, and dashes mighty waves against the rocks which receive them, and renders the haven very dangerous."*

Dr. KITTO says : "The fact is, the port is so dangerous, from exposure to the open sea, that the surf often rolls in with the utmost violence, and even so lately as 1842, a lieutenant and some sailors were lost in pulling to the shore from the English steamer that lay in the harbor."†

* Jewish War, B. iii. ch. 9.　　† Scripture Lands, p. 179.

The same author, in describing the situation of the town, says : "It chiefly faces the north, and the buildings appear, from the steepness of the site, as if standing upon one another." And again : "From the steepness of the site, many of the streets are connected by flights of steps, and the one that runs along the sea-wall is the most clean and regular of the whole."

The Baron GERAMB, a Trappist Monk, who visited the Holy Land in 1842, gives the following incident in connection with this subject :

"Yesterday morning, at day-break, boats pulled off and surrounded the vessel to take us to the town (of Joppa), the access to which is difficult, on account of the numerous rocks that present to view their bare flanks. The walls were covered with spectators, attracted by curiosity. The boats being much lower than the bridge, upon which one is obliged to climb, and, having no ladder, the landing is not effected without danger. More than once it has happened that passengers, in springing out, have broken their limbs, and we might have met with the like accident, *if several persons had not hastened to our assistance.*"

There can, therefore, be no doubt of the steepness of the shore at Joppa, and of the difficulty and danger to which the workmen, who navigated the floats from Tyre must have been exposed in landing ; and the authorities that we have quoted, wonderfully confirm the probability of the tradition on the subject contained in the Mark Master's degree.

EZEKIEL, xliv. 1, 5.

Then he brought me back the way of the gate of the outward sanctuary, which looketh toward the east ; and it was shut. And the Lord said unto me, Son of man, mark well, and behold with thine eyes and hear with thine ears, all that I say unto thee, concerning all the ordinances of the house of the Lord, and all the laws thereof; and mark well the entering in of the house, with every going forth of the sanctuary.

THE WORKING TOOLS.

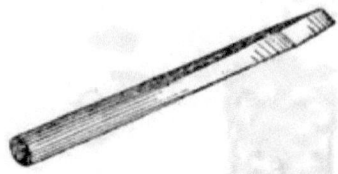 

The Chisel and Mallet are the working tools of a Mark Master, and are thus symbolically explained:

THE CHISEL

Morally demonstrates the advantages of discipline and education. The mind, like the diamond in its original state, is rude and unpolished; but as the effect of the chisel on the external coat soon presents to view the latent beauties of the diamond, so education discovers the latent virtues of the mind, and draws them forth to range the large field of matter and space, to display the summit of human knowledge, our duty to God and to man   .

THE MALLET

Morally teaches us to correct irregularities, and to reduce man to a proper level; so that, by quiet deportment he may, in the school of discipline, learn to be content. What the mallet is to the

2*

workman, enlightened reason is to the passions : it curbs ambition, it depresses envy, it moderates anger, and it encourages good dispositions; whence arises among good masons that comely order,

" Which nothing earthly gives, or can destroy,
The soul's calm sunshine, and the heartfelt joy."

The following passages of Scripture are here appropriately introduced :

ACTS, iv. 11.

" This is the stone which was set at nought of you builders, which is become the head stone of the corner."

REVELATIONS, ii. 17.

" To him that overcometh, will I give to eat of the hidden manna ; and I will give him a white stone, and in the stone a new name written, which no man knoweth, saving he that receiveth it."

REVELATIONS, iii. 13.

" He that hath an ear to hear, let him hear."

SYMBOLISM OF THE KEYSTONE.

The Keystone, in this degree, is evidently an allusion to the *tesseræ hospitales*, or hospitable tokens, among the ancients, which have already been spoken of, and which are thus described by Dr. ADAM CLARKE:

"A small oblong square piece of wood, bone, stone, or ivory, was taken, and divided into two equal parts, on which each of the parties wrote his own name, and then interchanged it with the other. This was carefully preserved, and handed down, even to posterity, in the same family; and by producing this when they traveled, it gave a mutual claim to the bearers of kind reception and hospitable entertainment at each other's houses."

In the passage from the second chapter of Revelations, which is read during the presentation of the Keystone, it is most probable that by the "white stone" and the "new name," St. John referred to these tokens of alliance and friendship. With these views, the symbolic allusion of the Keystone in the Mark degree is very apparent. It is intended to denote the firm and friendly alliance which exists between Mark Masters, and to indicate that by the possession of this token, and the new name inscribed upon it, and which is known only to those who have received it in the progress of their initiation, a covenant has been instituted that, in all future time, and under every circumstance of danger or distress, will secure the kind and friendly assistance of those who are the possessors of the same token. The Mark Master is thus, by the reception of this mystic sign, adopted into the fraternity of all other Mark Masons, and entitled to all the rights and privileges which belong exclusively to the partakers in the meaning of the same significant stone. The Keystone of a Mark Master is, therefore, the symbol of a fraternal covenant among those who are engaged in the common search after Divine Truth.

The following song is sung during the ceremonies of the degree:

MARK MASTER'S SONG.

Mark Mas - ters all ap - pear, Be - fore the
Chief O'er-seer, In con - cert move; Let him your
work ins-pect, For the Chief Arch - i - tect,
If there be no de - fect, He will ap - prove.

You who have pass'd the square,
For your rewards prepare,
  Join heart and hand;
Each with his mark in view,
March with the just and true;
Wages to you are due,
  At your command.

Hiram, the widow's son,
Sent unto Solomon
  Our great key-stone;
On it appears the name
Which raises high the fame
Of all to whom the same
  Is truly known.

Now to the westward move,
Where, full of strength and love,
  Hiram doth stand;
But if impostors are
Mix'd with the worthy there,
Caution them to beware
  Of the right hand.

Ceremonies.

Now to the praise of those
Who triumph'd o'er the foes
  Of mason's art;
To the praiseworthy three,
Who founded this degree;
May all their virtues be
  Deep in our hearts.

THE WAGES OF THE CRAFT.

THE traditions of Masonry respecting the wages of the workmen at the temple, instruct us that there were two divisions of the Fellow Crafts. The first, or higher class, were employed in the quarries, in hewing, squaring and numbering the stones, and thus preparing them for the builders' use; and that each one might be enabled to designate his own work, and to determine the amount of compensation which was due him, he was in possession of a mark, which he placed upon all the materials prepared by him. Hence this class of Fellow Crafts were called Mark Masters, and received their pay from the Senior Grand Warden, whom some suppose to have been Adoniram, the brother-in-law of Hiram Abif, and the first of the Provosts and Judges. They received their pay in money, at the rate of a half shekel of silver, equal to about twenty-five cents. They were paid weekly, at the sixth hour of the sixth day of the week—that is to say, on Friday, at noon.

The second, and probably larger class of the Fellow Crafts were younger and less experienced men, whose skill and knowledge were not such as to entitle them to advancement to the grade of Mark Master. These workmen were not, therefore, in possession of a mark, and proved their right to reward by another token. They received their wages in the middle chamber, and were paid in corn, wine, and oil, agreeably to the stipulation of King Solomon with Hiram, King of Tyre.

The promotion of a certain number of the Fellow Crafts to a higher degree, which was to be considered as an *honorarium*, or reward bestowed upon them for their superior skill and knowledge in their profession, has occasioned this degree to receive the technical title of "the honorary degree of a Mark Master," a term which Webb has in one place carelessly corrupted into "honorable."

The following passage from the Book of the Law is read:

MATTHEW xx. 1, 16.

"For the kingdom of heaven is like unto a man that is an householder, which went out early in the morning to hire labourers into his vineyard. And when he had agreed with the labourers for a penny a day, he sent them into his vineyard. And he went out about the third hour, and saw others standing idle in the market place, and said unto them, Go ye also into the vineyard, and whatsoever is right, I will give you. And they went their way. And again he went out about the sixth and ninth hour, and did likewise. And about the eleventh hour, he went out and found others standing idle, and saith unto them, Why stand ye here all the day idle? They say unto him, Because no man hath hired us. He saith unto them, Go ye also into the vineyard, and whatsoever is right, that shall ye receive. So when even was come, the lord of the vineyard saith unto his steward, Call the labourers, and give them their hire, beginning from the last unto the first. And when they came, that were hired about the eleventh hour, they received every man a penny. But when the first came, they supposed that they should have received more, and they likewise received every man a penny. And when they received it, they murmured against the good man of the house, saying, These last have wrought but one hour, and thou hast made them equal unto us, which have borne the burden and heat of the day. But he answered one of them, and said, Friend, I do thee no wrong; didst thou not agree with me for a penny? Take that thine is, and go thy way; I will give unto this last even as unto thee. Is it not lawful for me to do what I will with my own? Is thine eye evil, because I am good? So the last shall be first, and the first last: for many be called, but few chosen."

THE SYMBOLISM OF THE PARABLE.

THERE is no passage of Scripture recited in any portion of our ritual which is more appropriate to the ceremonies into which it is introduced, than is this sublime parable of our Lord to the whole extent and design of the Mark Master's Degree. We learn from it that the Grand Architect of the

Universe will make no distinction of persons in the distribution of His beneficence, but will give alike to each who sincerely seeks to obey the great law of His creation. Masonry regards no man on account of his worldly wealth or honors. It is the internal, and not the external qualifications that recommend a man to be a mason. No matter what may be the distinctions of place or office, the humblest shall receive as full a reward as the highest, if he has labored faithfully and effectually in the task set before him. And this arises from the very nature of the institution.

The lodge is the mason's vineyard; his labor is study, and his wages are *truth*. The youngest brother may, therefore, labor **more** earnestly than the oldest, and thus receive **more** light in Masonry as the reward of his earnest work. There was a young craftsman who had been idle all the week, doing no work whatsoever—the symbol of the profane, who has not yet been initiated into Masonry; yet, on the last day, at the eleventh **hour, he** found **in** the quarries and brought into the temple that stone which became the head of the corner. Thus did he more service to the house of the Lord than all those who had labored from the rising even to the setting of the sun, and yet who could offer no more at the end of each day's work than the ordinary result of **an ordi**nary man's labor.

The vineyard **of** Masonry is open to all. But he who works most diligently, though he began the latest, shall not be below him who, commencing earlier, has not put his whole heart into the task.

The design of all Masonry is the search after TRUTH, and every one who seeks to discover it, shall receive his reward in the attainment. However we may have endured the heat and burden of the day, if we have not labored wisely, with the true end in view—if our zeal has not been tempered with judgment—though first at the vineyard, we shall be last at the reward; for truth is to be found only by him who looks for it earnestly, and whose search **is** directed by wisdom, and supported by faithful courage and unfaltering zeal. It is not the time that you have been a mason, but the way in which that time has been employed, that will secure the prize of intellectual light. He who, like the youthful crafts-man in the quarries, has made one discovery in masonic science, is of more benefit as a member to the fraternity than he who, after long years, has learned nothing more than his ritual, just as the keystone **was** of infinitely more value than many ordinary blocks of stone.

So, then, let **us** all labor in the vineyard and the quarry—in the lodge and in the study—so that, being *called* as initi-ates to seek masonic truth, we also may be *chosen* to find it.

CHARGE.*

BROTHER : I congratulate you on having been thought worthy of being advanced to this honorary degree of Masonry. Permit me **to impress it on** your mind, that your assiduity should ever be com-mensurate with your duties, which become more and more extensive, as you advance in Masonry. In the honorable character of Mark Master Mason, it is more particularly your duty to endeavor to let your conduct in the lodge and among your brethren be such as may stand the test of the Great Over-seer's square ; that you may not, like the unfinished and imperfect work of the negligent and unfaithful of former times, be rejected and thrown aside, as

* This charge, first published, in a more complete form, by WEBB, is taken substantially, and, in some portions, with literal exactitude, from the charge contained in the ritual of the Mark Master Mason of the Ancient and Accepted Rite. I am indebted to the same ritual for the prayer which closes the degree.

unfit for that spiritual building—that house not made with hands—eternal in the heavens.

While such is your conduct, should misfortunes assail you, should friends forsake you, should envy traduce your good name, and malice persecute you, yet may you have confidence, that among Mark Master Masons you will find friends who will administer relief to your distresses and comfort to your afflictions, ever bearing in mind, as a consolation under all the frowns of fortune, and as an encouragement to hope for better prospects, that *the stone which the builders rejected*, possessing merits to them unknown, became the chief stone of the corner.

PRAYER

AT THE CLOSING OF A MARK MASTER'S LODGE.

Supreme Grand Architect of the Universe, who sitteth on the throne of mercy, deign to view our labors in the cause of virtue and humanity with the eye of compassion ; purify our hearts, and cause us to know and serve thee aright. Guide us in the paths of rectitude and honor ; correct our errors by the unerring square of thy wisdom, and enable us so to practice the precepts of Masonry, that all our actions may be acceptable in thy sight. *So mote it be. Amen.*

END OF THE MARK DEGREE.

BOOK II.

Past Master.

.

"Every association of men, as well as this of Freemasons, must, for the sake of order and harmony, be regulated by certain laws, and for that purpose, proper officers must be appointed and empowered to carry those laws into execution, to preserve a degree of uniformity, at least to restrain any irregularity that might render such associations inconsistent."

HUTCHINSON, SPIRIT OF MASONRY.

FIFTH DEGREE.

SYMBOLICAL DESIGN.

THE Past Master's degree presents us with a peculiar feature in the symbolism of the masonic system. While, as masons, we admit the general equality of men in their relation to their common Creator, and acknowledge with proper humility that we are all traveling on the level of time to " that undiscovered country from whose bourne no traveler returns," we do **not** deny the advantage and propriety of distinctions in society, based on a difference of talent, virtue and position ; and we know that while some must rule and govern, others must of necessity be called upon to obey. It is to this view of the gradations of society that the fifth degree alludes in its ceremonies and instructions. While the other degrees involve the duties and obligations of the various stages of human life, this degree confines itself to the consideration of only one aspect of these many duties. It is symbolic of the good, the wise, and the just ruler—whether it be of the sovereign **over** his people, **the** master over his household, or the father over his children.   It inculcates, by appropriate, yet singular, and sometimes unfortunately perverted ceremonies, the necessity of judgment, discretion, wisdom, firmness and determination in him who undertakes **to govern** his fellow-men, and of obedience, submission, order and discipline in those who would live happily **and** quietly under constituted authority.

HISTORICAL SUMMARY.

THIS degree was originally, and still is, in connection with Symbolic Masonry—an honorary degree conferred on the Master **of a lodge.   When a** brother, **who** has never before presided, has been elected the Master of a lodge, an Emergent Lodge **of Past** Masters, consisting of not less than three, is convened, and, all but **Past Masters** having **retired, the** degree is conferred upon the newly-elected officer ; **and this** conferring of the degree constitutes a part of the installation ceremony.

How long this custom has prevailed, we are **unable to determine ; but it is** probable that ever since the organization of the institution, some peculiar mark of distinction has been always bestowed upon those who were selected to rule over the craft.   The earliest written reference on this subject is found in the first edition of Anderson's Book of Constitutions.   A description is there given of the "manner of constituting a new lodge."   The Grand Master, after proclaiming the Master, is said to use " some other expressions that are proper and usual on that occasion, but not proper to be written."   From rituals of a not much later period that are in existence, **it** is evident that the author here refers to the very brief **mode of** conferring the Past Master's degree which was then in use, and which consisted of no more than a communication of the methods of recognition.

In Preston's time, the ceremonies had been enlarged, for he says, in describing the form of installation, that "the new Master is then conducted to an adjacent room, where he is regularly installed and bound to his trust in ancient form, in the presence of at least three installed Masters."

It is evident, then, that this degree was originally simply a degree of office, and conferred only on the elected Master of a lodge. As these rulers of Masonry were supposed to be selected for their superior skill and intelligence, they alone were permitted to receive that consummation of masonic light which is contained in the Royal Arch degree. Hence, therefore, the possession of the degree of Past Master became a necessary qualification for exaltation to the Royal Arch, and as, at first, that degree was conferred in connection with, and under the jurisdiction of, symbolic lodges, none but those who had presided in the chair were permitted to receive it.

So, in time, when the Chapters were separated from the lodges, and placed under a distinct jurisdiction, the usage still prevailed, and candidates for exaltation were invested, as a preparatory step, with the Past Master's degree, and for this purpose a lodge of Past Masters was opened, and a fictitious installation (for it was nothing else) was performed.

This was the origin of the insertion of this degree into the series of capitular degrees, which has in recent years occasioned so many almost bitter controversies respecting the contending rights of "actual" Past Masters, or those installed in a regularly constituted symbolic lodge, and "virtual" Past Masters made in a Chapter, simply as a qualification for receiving the Royal Arch degree.

One of the evils resulting from the disseverance of the Past Master's degree from its legitimate position as a part of the installation service in a symbolic lodge, was the introduction of a number of ceremonies into the Chapter degree, which were unknown to it in its original conception, and which are still unused in the installation of a Worshipful Master

These ceremonies became at length, by an unfortunate misdirection of the fertile genius of some inventor, so perverted from the original design of every masonic degree, which is to inculcate some particular moral or religious truth, as to meet with the very general condemnation of all intelligent and reflecting minds.

At length a powerful effort was made to divest the degree of those offensive ornaments which had been gradually fastened upon it, and to restore it, as nearly as possible, to its original simplicity. This effort was successful, and in September, 1856, the General Grand Chapter of the United States adopted a resolution, which recommended the subordinate Chapters under its jurisdiction " to abridge the ceremonies now conferred in the Past Master's degree within the narrowest constitutional limits, only retaining the inducting of the candidate into the Oriental Chair, and communicating the means of recognition."

It is to be hoped that this reform, dictated by good taste and judgment, will be approved and enforced by the presiding officers of all the Chapters.

The various sections of the lecture of this degree, which relate to the constitution of new lodges, the installation of officers, the laying of corner-stones, the dedication of halls, and the funeral service, being only necessary to the actual Past Masters of symbolic lodges, are of course omitted in this manual.

OPENING OF THE LODGE.

A Lodge of Past Masters consists, besides the Tiler, of the following seven officers

 Right Worshipful Master.

 Senior Warden.

 Junior Warden.

 Treasurer.

 Secretary.

 Senior Deacon.

 Junior Deacon.

These offices are filled by the officers of the Chapter under whose warrant the lodge is held, in the following order:

The High Priest, King, and Scribe, act as Master and Wardens; the Treasurer and Secretary occupy the corresponding stations; the Principal Sojourner acts as Senior Deacon; the Royal Arch Captain, as Junior Deacon.

The symbolic color of the Past Master's degree is purple. The apron is of white lamb-skin, edged with purple, and should have the jewel of the degree inscribed upon it. The collar is of purple, edged with gold. But, as Past Master's lodges are held under the warrants of Royal Arch Chapters, the collars, aprons and jewels of the Chapter are generally made use of in conferring the Past Master's degree.

The jewel of a Past Master is a pair of golden compasses, extended to sixty degrees, and resting on the fourth of a circle. Between the extended legs of the compasses is a flaming sun.*

Lodges of Past Masters are "dedicated to the Holy Saints John."

A candidate receiving this degree is said to be " seated in the Oriental chair of King Solomon."

PRAYER

ON OPENING A LODGE OF PAST MASTERS.

Most holy and glorious Lord God, the Great Architect of the universe, the Giver of all good gifts and graces : Thou hast promised, that where two or three are gathered together in thy name, thou wilt be in the midst of them, and bless them. In thy name we assemble, most humbly beseeching thee to bless us in all our undertakings, that we may know and serve thee aright, and that all our actions may tend to thy glory, and to our advancement in knowledge and virtue. And we beseech

---

* The jewel, in England, was formerly a square, resting on an arc of ninety degrees; at the present time it is the square, with a silver plate suspended within it, on which is engraved a diagram of the forty-seventh problem of Euclid.

thee, O Lord God, to bless our present assembling, and to illuminate our minds, that we may walk in the light of thy countenance ; and when the trials of our probationary state are over, be admitted into THE TEMPLE "not made with hands, eternal in the heavens." *So mote it be. Amen.*

RECEPTION.

Previous to the investiture of the candidate, he is, in many jurisdictions, required to signify his assent to the following charges. They are not, however, really necessary, and are somewhat out of place in conferring the degree in a Chapter. They are inserted, but their use is not recommended, except in the ceremony of installing the **actual** Master of a Symbolic Lodge :

BROTHER :—Previous to your investiture, it is necessary that you should signify your assent to those ancient charges and regulations which point out the duty of the Master of a lodge :

I. You agree to be a good man and true, and strictly to obey the moral law.

II. You agree to be a peaceable citizen, and cheerfully to conform to the laws of the country in which you reside.

III. You promise not to be concerned in plots and conspiracies against government, but patiently to submit to the decisions of the supreme legislature.

IV. You agree to pay a proper respect to the civil magistrates, to work diligently, live creditably, and act honorably by all men.

V. You agree to hold in veneration the original rulers and patrons of the order of Masonry, and their regular successors, supreme and subordinate, according to their stations ; and to submit to the awards and resolutions of your brethren, when convened, in every case consistent with the constitutions of the order.

VI. You agree to avoid private piques and quarrels, and to guard against intemperance and excess.

VII. You agree to be cautious in carriage and behavior, courteous to your brethren, and faithful to your lodge.

VIII. You promise to respect genuine brethren, and to discountenance impostors, and all dissenters from the original plan of Masonry.

IX. You agree to promote the general good of society, to cultivate the social virtues, and to propagate the knowledge of the art.

X. You promise to pay homage to the Grand Master for the time being, and to his officers when duly installed ; and strictly to conform to every edict of the Grand Lodge, or general assembly of masons, that is not subversive of the principles and groundwork of Masonry.

XI. You admit that it is not in the power of any man, or body of men, to make innovations in the body of Masonry.

XII. You promise a regular attendance on the committees and communications of the Grand Lodge, on receiving proper notice, and to pay attention to all the duties of Masonry, on convenient occasions.

XIII. You admit that no new lodge shall be formed without permission of the Grand Lodge, and that no countenance be given to an irregular lodge, or to any person clandestinely initiated therein, being contrary to the ancient charges of the order.

XIV. You admit that no person can be regularly made a mason in, or admitted a member of, any regular lodge, without previous notice, and due inquiry into his character.

XV. You agree that no visitors shall be received into your lodge without due examination, and producing proper vouchers of their having been initiated in a regular lodge.

These are the regulations of free and accepted masons.

Do you submit to these charges and promise to support these regulations, as Masters have done in all ages before you?

THE GIBLEMITES OR STONE-SQUARERS.

The Giblemites, or, as they are called in Scripture, the *Giblim*, were inhabitants of the city and district of Gebal, in Phœnicia, near Mount Lebanon, and were, therefore, under the dominion of the King of Tyre. The Phœnician word "*gibal*," which makes "*giblim*" in the plural, signifies a mason or stone-squarer. In the Second Book of Kings, chapter v., and verses 17 and 18, we read that "the King commanded, and they brought great stones, costly stones, and hewed stones, to lay the foundation of the house. And Solomon's builders and Hiram's builders did hew them, and the stone-squarers," which last word is, in the original, *giblim*. Gesenius* says that the inhabitants of Gebal were seamen and builders, and Sir William Drummond† asserts that "the Gibalim were Master Masons, who put the finishing hand to Solomon's temple." In this sense the word is also used in the Book of Constitutions,‡ which records that John de Spoulee, who, as one of the deputies of Edward III., assisted in rebuilding Windsor Castle, was called the "Master of the Ghiblim." The Giblim, or the Giblimites, were, therefore, stone-squarers or Master Masons.

————•————

IMPLEMENTS OF A PAST MASTER.

The implements necessary to a Present or Past Master are sometimes presented to the candidate, and their uses explained.

* Hebrew Lexicon in voce.   † Origines, vol. iii., b. 5, ch. iv., p. 192.
‡ Anderson's Constitutions, edition 1738, p. 70.

The Book of the Law, that great light in Masonry, will guide you to all truth ; it will direct your path to the temple of happiness, and point out to you the whole duty of man.

The *Square* teaches us to regulate our actions by rule and line, and to harmonize our conduct by the principles of morality and virtue.

The *Compasses* teach us to limit our desires in every station—that, rising to eminence by merit, we may live respected and die regretted.

The *Rule* directs that we should punctually observe our duty, press forward in the path of virtue, and, neither inclining to the right nor to the left, in all our actions have eternity in view.

The *Line* teaches the criterion of moral rectitude,

3*

to avoid dissimulation in conversation and action, and to direct our steps to the path which leads to a glorious immortality.

The *Book of Constitutions* you are to search at all times. Cause it to be read in your lodge, that none may pretend ignorance of the excellent precepts it enjoins.

You now receive in charge the *Charter*, by the authority of which this lodge is held. You are carefully to preserve and duly transmit it to your successors in office.

You will also receive in charge the *By-Laws* of your lodge, which you are to see carefully and punctually executed.

The ceremonies may be concluded by the delivery to the candidate of the following explanatory

CHARGE.

BROTHER:—The conferring at this time of a degree which has no historical connection with the other capitular degrees, is an apparent anomaly, which, however, is indebted for its existence to the following circumstances :

Originally, when Royal Arch Masonry was under the government of symbolic lodges, in which the Royal Arch degree was then always conferred, it was a regulation that no one could receive it unless he had previously presided as the Master of that or some other lodge ; and this restriction was made because the Royal Arch was deemed too important a degree to be conferred only on Master Masons.

But, as by confining the Royal Arch to those only who had been actually elected as the presiding officers of their lodges, the extension of the degree would have been materially circumscribed, and its usefulness greatly impaired, the Grand Master often granted, upon due petition, his dispensation to permit certain Master Masons (although not elected to preside over their lodges) *"to pass the chair,"* which was a technical term, intended to designate a brief ceremony, by which the candidate was invested with the mysteries of a Past Master, and, like him, entitled to advance in Masonry as far as the Royal

Arch, or the perfection and consummation of the third degree.

When, however, the control of the Royal Arch was taken from the symbolic lodges and entrusted to a distinct organization—that, namely, of Chapters—the regulation continued to be observed, for it was doubtful to many whether it could legally be abolished; and, as the law still requires that the august degree of Royal Arch shall be restricted to Past Masters, our candidates are made to pass the chair simply as a preparation and qualification toward being invested with the solemn instructions of the Royal Arch.

The ceremony of passing the chair, or making you in this manner a Past Master, does not, however, confer upon you any official rank outside of the Chapter, nor can you in a symbolic lodge claim any peculiar privileges in consequence of your having received in the Chapter the investiture of the Past Master's degree. Those who receive the degree in symbolic lodges as a part of the installation service, when elected to preside, have been properly called "Actual Past Masters," while those who pass through the ceremony in a Chapter, as simply preparatory to taking the Royal Arch, are distinguished as "Virtual Past Masters," to show that, with the investiture of the secrets, they have not received the rights and prerogatives of the degree.

With this brief explanation of the reason why this degree is now conferred upon you, and why you have been permitted to occupy the chair, you will retire, and suffer yourself to be prepared for those further and profounder researches into Masonry, which can only be consummated in the Royal Arch degree.

PRAYER

AT CLOSING A LODGE OF PAST MASTERS.

Supreme Architect of the Universe, accept our humble praises for the many mercies and blessings which thy bounty has conferred on us, and especially for this friendly and social intercourse. Pardon, we beseech thee, whatever thou hast seen amiss in us, since we have been together ; and continue to us thy presence, protection and blessing. Make us sensible of the renewed obligations we are under to love thee supremely, and to be friendly to each other. May all our irregular passions be subdued, and may we daily increase in *Faith, Hope* and *Charity*, but more especially in that *Charity* which is the bond of peace, and the perfection of every virtue. May we so practise thy precepts, that we may finally obtain thy promises, and find an entrance through the gates into the temple and city of our God. *So mote it be. Amen.*

END OF THE PAST MASTER'S DEGREE.

BOOK III.

Most Excellent Master.

"The ever-memorable occasion of the dedication of the temple is celebrated in our lodges. It is the groundwork of one of its most beautiful degrees. It has been celebrated for thousands of generations, and is hallowed in the memory of the craft."

SCOTT'S ANALOGY.

SIXTH DEGREE.

SYMBOLICAL DESIGN.

THE sixth degree, or that of Most Excellent Master, is as intimately connected with the third or Master Mason's as the Mark Master's is with that of the Fellow Craft. The Master Mason's degree is intended, in its symbolic design, to teach the doctrines of the resurrection of the dead and the immortality of the soul. But this corruption can only put on incorruption, and this mortal put on immortality by a passage through the portals of the grave. And here the degree of Most Excellent Master comes forward with its beautiful symbolism, to represent the man prepared to enter upon that eventful passage. In the preceding degrees the duties of life have been delineated under various types—the virtuous craftsman has been assiduously laboring to erect within his heart a spiritual temple of holiness, fit for the habitation of Him who is the holiest of beings. If the moral and religious

(65)

precepts of the order have been observed, stone has been placed upon stone—virtue has been added to virtue—and the duties of one day have been scrupulously performed, only that the duties of the next may be commenced with equal zeal.

And now all is accomplished—the spiritual edifice which it was given to man to erect—that "house not made with hands, eternal in the heavens"—upon the construction of which he has been engaged, day by day and hour by hour, from his first entrance into the world—has become a stately and finished building, and there remains no more to be done, save to place the cape-stone, DEATH, upon its summit.

This—the last condition of man on earth, when all his labors have been completed—when he is about to lay aside for ever all his projects of ambition, of pleasure, or of business—to dissolve the ties which have bound him to the companions of his toils, and to go forth a wanderer on the unknown shores of eternity—to abandon, as useless, the implements of this world's work, and to leave the temple of life—is the solemn scene which is symbolically commemorated in the impressive ceremonies of the Most Excellent Master's degree.

HISTORICAL SUMMARY.

The legend or tradition upon which the degree of Most Excellent Master is founded, is thus recorded in the Book of Constitutions :*

"The temple was finished in the short space of seven years and six months, to the amazement of all the world; when the cape-stone was celebrated by the fraternity with great joy. But their joy was soon interrupted by the sudden

* Anderson's Constitutions, second edition, 1738, p. 14.

death of their dear master, Hiram Abif, whom they decently interred in the lodge near the temple, according to ancient usage.

"After Hiram Abif was mourned for, the tabernacle of Moses and its holy relics being lodged in the temple, Solomon, in a general assembly, dedicated or consecrated it by solemn prayer and costly sacrifices past number, with the finest music, vocal and instrumental, praising Jehovah, upon fixing the holy ark in its proper place between the cherubim; when Jehovah filled his own temple with a cloud of glory."

The ceremonies commemorated in this degree, refer, therefore, to the completion and dedication of the temple. It is reasonable to suppose that, when this magnificent edifice was completed, King Solomon should bestow some distinguished mark of his approval upon the skillful and zealous builders who had been engaged for seven years in its construction. No greater token of that approbation could have been evinced than to establish an order of merit, with the honorable appellation of "Most Excellent Masters," and to bestow it upon those of the craftsmen who had proved themselves to be complete masters of their profession. It was not conferred upon the whole body of the workmen but was confined, as Webb remarks, to the meritorious and praiseworthy—to those who, through diligence and industry, had progressed far toward perfection. Such is the traditional history of the origin of the degree. And it is still retained as a memorial of the method adopted by the wise King of Israel to distinguish the most faithful and skillful portion of his builders, and to reward them for their services by receiving and acknowledging them as Most Excellent Masters, at the completion and dedication of the temple.

THE TEMPLE OF SOLOMON.

As this degree refers to that important period when the temple erected by King Solomon for the worship of Jehovah was completed, and presented in all its glory and beauty to an admiring people, it is proper that the masonic student should here receive some brief details of this magnificent structure.

Mount Moriah, on which the foundations of the temple were laid, was a lofty hill, situated almost in the very north-east corner of the city of Jerusalem, having Mount Zion on the south-west, with the city of David and the king's palace on its summit, and Mount Acra on the west, whereon the lower city was built.

The summit of the mountain on which the temple was built, which, although not very high, was exceedingly steep, occupied a square of five hundred cubits, or two hundred and fifty yards on each side, being encompassed by a stone wall one thousand yards in extent, and twelve yards and a half high.

King Solomon commenced the erection of the temple on the second day of the Hebrew month Zif, in the year of the world 2992, which date corresponds to Monday, the first of April, 1012 years before the Christian era.

The foundations were laid at a profound depth, and consisted, as Josephus informs us, of stones of immense size and great durability. They were closely mortised into the rock, so as to form a secure basis for the superincumbent structure.

The building does not appear to have been so remarkable for its magnitude as for the magnificence of its ornaments and the value of its materials. LIGHTFOOT gives us the best idea of its size and form when he says that the porch was one hundred and twenty cubits, or two hundred and ten feet high and that the rest of the building was in height but thirty cubits, or fifty-two feet and a half, so that the form of the

whole house was thus: It was situated due east and west,
the holy of holies being to the westward, and the porch or
entrance toward the east. The whole length from east to
west, was seventy cubits, or one hundred and twenty-two
feet and a half. The breadth, exclusive of the side chambers,
was twenty cubits, or thirty-five feet; the height of the holy
place and the holy of holies was thirty cubits, or fifty-two
feet and a half, and the porch stood at the eastern end, like
a lofty steeple, one hundred and twenty cubits, or two hun-

dred and ten feet high.   In fact, as LIGHTFOOT remarks, the temple much resembled a modern church, with this difference, that the steeple which was placed over the porch was situated at the east end.*

Around the north and south sides and the west end were built chambers of three stories, each story being five cubits in height, or fifteen cubits, twenty-six feet nine inches in all—and these were united to the outside wall of the house.

The windows, which were used for ventilation rather than for light, which was derived from the sacred candlesticks, were placed in the wall of the temple that was above the roof of the side chambers. But that part which included the holy of holies was without any aperture whatever, to which Solomon alludes in the passage, "The Lord said that He would dwell in the thick darkness."

The temple was divided, internally, into three parts—the porch, the sanctuary, and the holy of holies; the breadth of all these was of course the same, namely, twenty cubits, or thirty-five feet, but they differed in length. The porch was seventeen feet six inches in length, the sanctuary seventy feet, and the holy of holies thirty-five, or, in the Hebrew measure, ten, forty, and twenty cubits. The entrance from the porch into the sanctuary was through a wide door of olive posts and leaves of fir; but the door between the sanctuary and the holy of holies was composed entirely of olive wood. These doors were always open, and the aperture closed by a suspended curtain. The partition between the sanctuary and the holy of holies partly consisted of an open network, so that the incense daily offered in the former place might be diffused through the interstices into the latter.

In the sanctuary were placed the golden candlestick, the table of shew bread, and the altar of incense. The holy of

* LIGHTFOOT'S "Prospect of the Temple," opp. vol. ix., p. 247.   The engraving here given is taken from SAMUEL LEE's "Orbis Miraculum," a rare and valuable description of the temple of Solomon. It gives a rude but accurate idea of the form of the body of the temple.

holies contained nothing but the ark of the covenant, which included the tables of the law.

The framework of the temple consisted of massive stone, but it was wainscoted with cedar, which was covered with gold. The boards within the temple were ornamented with carved work, skillfully representing cherubim, palm leaves and flowers. The ceiling of the temple was supported by beams of cedar wood, which, with that used in the wainscoting, was supplied by the workmen of Hiram, King of Tyre, from the forest of Lebanon. The floor was throughout made of cedar, but boarded over with planks of fir.

The temple, thus constructed, was surrounded by various courts and high walls, and thus occupied the entire summit of Mount Moriah. The first of the Courts was the court of the Gentiles, beyond which Gentiles were prohibited from passing. Within this, and separated from it by a low wall, was the Court of the Children of Israel, and inside of that, separated from it by another wall, was the Court of the Priests, in which was placed the altar of burnt offerings. From this court there was an ascent of twelve steps to the porch of the temple, before which stood the two pillars of Jachin and Boaz.

For the erection of this magnificent structure, besides the sums annually appropriated by Solomon, his father, David, had left one hundred thousand talents of gold, and a million talents of silver, equal to nearly four thousand millions of dollars.*

The time occupied in its construction was seven years and about six months, and it was finished in the month Bul, in the year of the world 3000, corresponding to October, 1004, of the vulgar era. The year after, it was dedicated with

---

* According to the accurate tables of Arbuthnot, reduced to Federal currency, a talent of gold is equal to $24,309, and a talent of silver to $1505,62,5. Hence, a hundred thousand talents of gold—$2,430,900,000, and a million talents—$1,505,625 000, and the whole—$3,936,525,000, the exact amount of gold and silver left by David for building the temple.

those solemn ceremonies which are alluded to in this degree.
The dedicatory ceremonies commenced on Friday, the 30th
of October, and lasted for fourteen days, terminating on
Thursday, the 12th of November, although the people were
not dismissed until the following Saturday. Seven days of
this festival were devoted to the dedication exclusively, and
the remaining seven to the Feast of Tabernacles which followed. The eighth chapter of the First Book of Kings
contains an account of the solemnities of the occasion, and
to that the reader is referred.

THE DEDICATION OF THE TEMPLE.

THE celebration of the cape-stone is a phrase which really
signifies the dedication of the temple, the ceremonies of
which are commemorated in this degree.

A dedication is defined to be a religious ceremony, where-
by anything is dedicated or consecrated to the service of
God. It appears, **says KITTO,** to have originated in the desire
to commence, with peculiar solemnity, the practical use and
application of whatever had been set apart to the Divine
service. Thus Moses dedicated the tabernacle in the wilderness; Solomon his temple; the returned exiles theirs, and
Herod his.

Not only, says the same author, were sacred places thus
dedicated, but some kind of dedicatory solemnity was
observed with respect to cities, walls, gates, and even private houses. We may trace the continuance of these usages
in the custom of consecrating or dedicating churches and
chapels, and in the ceremonies connected with the opening
of roads, markets, bridges, &c., and with the launching of
ships.*

* Kitto's Biblical Cyclopedia.

OPENING OF THE LODGE.

A LODGE of Most Excellent Masters consists, besides the Tiler, of the following seven officers:

> MOST EXCELLENT MASTER.
>
> SENIOR WARDEN.
>
> JUNIOR WARDEN.
>
> TREASURER.
>
> SECRETARY.
>
> SENIOR DEACON.
>
> JUNIOR DEACON.

These offices are filled by the officers of the Chapter under whose warrant the lodge is held, in the following order:

The High Priest, King, and Scribe, act as Master and Warden; the Treasurer and Secretary occupy the corresponding stations; the Principal Sojourner acts as Senior Deacon, and the Royal Arch Captain, as Junior Deacon.

The Most Excellent Master represents King Solomon, and should be dressed in a crimson robe, wearing a crown, and holding a sceptre in his hand.

The symbolic color of the Most Excellent Master's degree is purple. The apron is of white lambskin, edged with purple. The collar is of purple, edged with gold. But, as lodges of this degree are held under warrants of Royal Arch Chapters, the collars, aprons and jewels of the Chapter are generally made use of in conferring the degree.

Lodges of Most Excellent Masters are "dedicated to King Solomon."

A candidate receiving this degree is said to be "received and acknowledged as a Most Excellent Master." This alludes

4

to the reception into the degree by King Solomon, and his acknowledgment of the skill and merits of those upon whom, at the completion and dedication of the temple, he is said to have originally conferred it.

The following Psalm is read at the **opening**:

PSALM xxiv.

The earth is the Lord's and the fullness thereof; the world, and they that dwell therein. For he hath founded it upon the seas, and established it upon the floods. Who shall ascend into the hill of the Lord? or who shall stand in his holy place? He that hath clean hands, and a pure heart; who hath not lifted up his soul unto vanity, nor sworn deceitfully. He shall receive the blessing from the Lord, and righteousness from the God of his salvation. This is the generation of them that seek him, that seek thy face, O Jacob: Lift up your heads, O ye gates; and be ye lifted up, ye everlasting doors, and the King of Glory shall come in. Who is this King of Glory? The Lord, strong and mighty; the Lord, mighty in battle. Lift up your heads, O ye gates; even lift them up, ye everlasting doors, and the King of Glory shall come in. Who is this King of Glory? The Lord of Hosts, he is the King of Glory.

This Psalm is peculiarly appropriate to the opening ceremonies of the Most Excellent Master's degree. One of the most important events referred to in this degree is the bringing forth of the ark of the covenant " with shouting and praise," and depositing it in the holy of holies, which was done at the dedication of the temple by King Solomon. So the twenty-fourth Psalm was originally composed and sung when David brought up the ark, with great pomp and procession, from the house of Obed-edom, and placed it in the tabernacle on Mount Zion. The two events were analogous, and hence the appropriateness of selecting the sacred song used on the one occasion as a preface to the ceremonies of a degree which commemorates the other.

RECEPTION.

The following Psalm is read during the ceremony of reception :

PSALM CXXII.

I was glad when they said unto me, Let us go into the house of the Lord.

Our feet shall stand within thy gates, O Jerusalem. Jerusalem is builded as a city that is compact together.

Whither the tribes go up, the tribes of the Lord, unto the testimony of Israel, to give thanks unto the name of the Lord.

For there are set thrones of judgment, the thrones of the house of David.

Pray for the peace of Jerusalem ; they shall prosper that love thee. **Peace be within thy walls, and** prosperity within thy palaces.

For my brethren **and** companions' sakes, **I will** now say, Peace be within thee. Because **of the** house of the Lord our God I will seek thy good.

A MOST EXCELLENT MASTER.

THE Hebrews had three titles of honor, each differing from the other in degree, which they bestowed upon their teachers and eminent men, and which KITTO compares to the modern collegiate designations of Bachelor, Master and Doctor :

1. *Rab*, which signified a great one, a chief, a master.

2. *Rabbi*, which, by the addition of the suffix *i* to the former, literally denotes " my master," but, as a title of higher dignity, may be said to signify " an Excellent Master."

3. *Rabboni*, " my great master," from *raban*, a great master, still higher than *rabbi*, and to be translated most appropriately as " a Most Excellent Master."

This was the title given in John xx. 16, by Mary to the Saviour : " She turned herself, and saith unto him, Rabboni."

HOFFMANN says, in the Chronicles of Cartaphilus, that *Rabboni* imports a higher title of respect than *Rab* or *Rabbi*, and confers the highest possible distinction in respect to wisdom and learning—so much so, that it is said to be conceded only to seven persons recorded in all Jewish history.

THE QUEEN OF SHEBA.

THE visit of the Queen of Sheba to King Solomon is recorded in the tenth chapter of the First Book of Kings, where we are told that " when the Queen of Sheba heard of the fame of Solomon concerning the name of the Lord, she came to prove him with hard questions ;" and we are further informed that when she " had seen all Solomon's wisdom and the house that he built, there was no spirit in her," which expression Dr. CLARKE properly interprets as meaning that " she was overpowered with astonishment."

The masonic legend coincides with this account, although there are one or two circumstances detailed in the tradition which have not been preserved in the written record.

According to the masonic tradition, we learn that the wide-spread reputation of King Solomon induced the Queen of Sheba, a country supposed by most commentators to be situated in the southern part of Arabia, to visit Jerusalem, and inspect the celebrated works of which she had heard so many encomiums. And we are informed that when she first beheld the magnificent edifice, which glittered with gold, and seemed, from the nice adjustments and exact accuracy of all its joints, to be composed of but a single piece of marble, she raised her eyes and hands in an attitude of admiration, and exclaimed, " Rabboni," which, being interpreted, means " a Most Excellent Master."

According to the received Bible chronology, the visit of
the Queen of Sheba to Solomon took place thirteen years
after the dedication of the temple, and objection has hence
been made to any allusion to her in the ceremonies which
refer to that dedication. But the objection is an unreasonable one, and is founded on an erroneous view of the nature
of masonic degrees. The ceremonies of the degree, as we
now have them, are not to be supposed to be the invention
of King Solomon, or to have been known in his day. They
are but a memorial, subsequently established, (at what later
period we know not,) of the events which occurred at the
temple. The Queen of Sheba, if Scripture record is to be
believed, must have expressed her admiration of the temple
when she first beheld it, though many years after its completion ; and it is allowable that that admiration should be
afterwards referred to when the memorial ceremonies were
adopted, and that it should even supply the basis of a means
of recognition, which it is by no means necessary to believe
was contemporary with the dedication. In all such cases, it
must be remembered that all masonic degrees are but
memorial ceremonies of the events which actually occurred
at the temple, and which, by means of these subsequently
adopted ceremonies, have been orally handed down to the
craft. This rational theory will meet all such objections as
the allusion to the Queen of Sheba in this degree, the use
of a New Testament parable in the Mark Master's, or the
reading of a passage from Ecclesiastes in the Master Mason's. By this theory these apparent anachronisms are easily explained, and they cannot be otherwise.

THE DAY SET APART FOR THE CELEBRATION OF THE CAPE-STONE OF THE TEMPLE.

THE CAPE-STONE, or, as it would more correctly be called, the cope-stone, (but the former word has been consecrated to us by universal masonic usage,) is the topmost stone of a building. To bring it forth, therefore, and to place it in its destined position, is significative that the building is completed, which event is celebrated, even by the operative masons of the present day, with great signs of rejoicing. Flags are hoisted on the top of every edifice by the builders engaged in its construction, as soon as they have reached the topmost post, and thus finished their labors. This is the "celebration of the cape-stone"—the celebration of the completion of the building—when their tools are laid aside, and rest and refreshment succeed for a time to labor. This is the event in the history of the temple which is commemorated in this degree. *The day set apart for the celebration of the cape-stone of the temple*, is the day devoted to rejoicing and thanksgiving for the completion of that glorious structure.

Masonic teachers have not agreed in determining what was the particular stone referred to in this degree. A few suppose it to have represented the last and highest stone placed in the temple. If this were the case, the Mark Master's keystone would be very improperly made use of on this occasion, for it by no means represents the highest stone of the temple. A majority of scholars have, however, adopted the more consistent theory that the keystone was appropriately used in this degree, and that it was deposited on the day of the completion of the temple in the place for which it was intended, all of which relates to a mystery not unfolded in this degree, but reserved for that of Select Master. In either case it was a cape-stone—in one, the cape-stone of the whole temple; in the other, only of an important part of it.

In my own recollection, a promise of secrecy was exacted of all Most Excellent Masters respecting the place where the keystone was deposited, and, although this usage has now very generally been abandoned, I have the most satisfactory reasons for knowing that such a promise constituted a part of the original OB. of the degree.

BRINGING FORTH THE ARK OF THE COVENANT WITH SHOUTING AND PRAISE.

PREVIOUS to the building of the temple, David had brought the ark of the covenant from the house of Obed-edom to his palace on Mount Zion, where it remained until the temple was completed.

As soon as Solomon had finished his work, he assembled the people, with their rulers and elders, at Jerusalem, that they might dedicate it with appropriate ceremonies. The ark was then taken from the palace of David and removed to the temple. The king himself and all the people and Levites went before, rendering the ground moist, says Josephus, with sacrifices and drink offerings, and the blood of a great number of oblations, and burning an immense quantity of incense, and thus with singing and dancing was it carried into the temple. But when it was to be transferred to the holy of holies, the rest of the multitude departed, and only those priests who bore it by its staves entered within the sacred place, and set it between the two cherubim, which, embracing it between their wings, covered it as with a dome.

It is this bringing of the ark into the temple with shouting and praise, and depositing it in the holy spot where it was thenceforth to remain, that is commemorated by a portion of the ceremonies of the Most Excellent Master's degree.

The following Ode is sung, accompanied with appropriate ceremonies:

MOST EXCELLENT MASTER'S SONG.

All hail to the morning, that bids us re-joice;

The tem-ple's com-plet-ed ex-alt high each voice, The

cape-stone is finish-ed, our la-bor is o'er; The

sound of the ga-vel shall hail us no more. To the

pow - er Al - migh-ty, who   ev - er has   gui - ded the

tribes of   old   Is - rael,   ex - alt - ing their fame;

To   him who hath   governed   our hearts un - di - vi - ded

Let's send forth our   voi - ces   to   praise his   great name.

Companions assemble
  On this joyful day,
(The occasion is glorious,)
  The keystone to lay;
Fulfill'd is the promise,
  By the ANCIENT OF DAYS,
To bring forth the cape-stone
  With shouting and praise.

Ceremonies.

There is no more occasion for level or plumb-line,
For trowel or gavel, for compass or square;
Our works are completed, the ark safely seated,
And we shall be greeted as workmen most rare.

    Now those that are worthy,
      Our toils who have shar'd,
    And prov'd themselves faithful,
      Shall meet their reward.
    Their virtue and knowledge,
      Industry and skill,
    Have our approbation,
      Have gained our good will.

We accept and receive them, Most Excellent Masters,
Invested with honors, and power to preside;
Among worthy craftsmen, wherever assembled,
The knowledge of masons to spread far and wide.

ALMIGHTY JEHOVAH!
    Descend now and fill
This lodge with thy glory,
    Our hearts with good-will!
Preside at our meetings,
    Assist us to find
True pleasure in teaching
    Good-will to mankind.

Thy *wisdom* inspired the great institution,
    Thy *strength* shall support it till nature expire;
And when the creation shall fall into ruin,
    Its *beauty* shall rise through the midst of the fire!

The following, which is a portion of the prayer of King Solomon at the dedication of the temple, may be used during this part of the ceremony:

PRAYER.

And now, O God of Israel, let thy word, I pray thee, be verified, which thou spakest unto thy servant David, my father. But will God indeed dwell on the earth? Behold, the heaven and heaven of heavens cannot contain thee; how much less this house that I have built. Yet have thou respect unto the prayer of thy servant, and to his supplication, O Lord my God, to hearken unto the cry and to the prayer which thy servant prayeth before thee to-day: that thine eyes may be open toward this house night and day, even toward the place of which thou hast said, My name shall be there: that thou mayest hearken unto the prayer which thy servant shall make toward this place. And hearken thou to the supplication of thy servant, and of thy people, Israel, when they shall pray toward this place; and hear thou in heaven, thy dwelling-place; and when thou hearest, forgive. *So mote it be. Amen.*

The following is read with solemn ceremonies:

II. Chronicles vii. 1–4.

Now when Solomon had made an end of praying, the fire came down from heaven, and consumed the burnt offering and sacrifices; and the glory of the Lord filled the house. And the priest could not enter into the house of the Lord, because the glory of the Lord had filled the Lord's house.

And when all the children of Israel saw how the fire came down, and the glory of the Lord upon the house, they bowed themselves with their faces to the ground upon the pavement, and worshiped, and praised the Lord, saying, For he is good; for his mercy endureth for ever.

THE FIRE FROM HEAVEN.

The following passages from Bro. Scott's "Analogy," *
may be advantageously read by the masonic student in
reference to this period of the ceremonies:

"It was when Solomon had made an end of praying, that
the fire came down from heaven; but it was before the fire
came down that the cloud of God's **glory** descended, and
that the Almighty was made manifest in the **sanctum sanctorum**. It was on the day of dedication, **and** the year of
dedication was a jubilee. The silver trumpets had ushered
it in amidst the rejoicing of all the people. The elders **of
Israel** had been assembled in the devoted city of Jerusalem.
Solomon had summoned them to meet together for **a holy**
purpose. **The stately** temple was completed. It **towered in**
all its grandeur. **It** was the wonder and **admiration of the**
world. **The** craftsmen were all present at **the** dedication.

> They had no more occasion for level or plumb-line,
> For trowel or gavel, for compass or square.

"Their work was all finished, and the ark of the covenant
was about to be brought up 'out of the city of David, which
is Zion.' How sublime and surpassingly grand were the ceremonies of dedication. 'And all the elders of Israel came, and
the priests took up the ark.' And the tabernacle was carried
up also, and all the holy vessels that were in it. Then the sacrifices commenced. All the congregation of Israel took part
in the ceremonies. The sheep and the oxen to be sacrificed
were numberless. When the ark was borne into 'the oracle of
the house, to the most holy place,' the cherubim spread forth
their wings over the place and covered the ark and the staves
thereof. And when it was safely seated, Almighty Jehovah
descended and filled the house with his glory. Yes, the Lord
was visible there; and well might the wisest of men, in the

---

* The Analogy of Ancient Craft Masonry to Natural and Revealed Religion, by Charles Scott, A.M., p. 217.

presence of all the congregation of Israel, pour out a fervent and most eloquent prayer to Him for his multiplied blessings. What a mighty assembly had gathered together! The Lord of heaven and earth was there. And never before had such eloquence fallen from the lips of Solomon. His prayer is a specimen of true devotion, and of what a wise man can do and say, 'when out of the abundance of the heart the mouth speaketh.'

"That ever memorable occasion is celebrated in our lodges. It is the ground-work of one of its most beautiful degrees. It has been celebrated for thousands of generations, and is hallowed in the memory of the craft. And may we not, with propriety, say that the splendid and eloquent prayer of our Grand Master, although it is not expressly incorporated into the regular body of masonry, constitutes, by implication, a portion of our institution? If we are correct in the opinion that our order was perfected at the completion of the temple, or even established after that period, but associated with the progress of that building and dedication, then we may very reasonably contend that every rite or event connected with it affords a subject for masonic study and investigation."

There is also an eloquent description of the scene commemorated in this degree in Dr. Jarvis's "Church of the Redeemed," pp. 166–168, which the masonic student may read with advantage and pleasure.

THE RECEPTION AND ACKNOWLEDGMENT.

Masonic tradition informs us that when the temple had been completed and dedicated, and the cape-stone celebrated, King Solomon *received and acknowledged* the most expert of the craftsmen as Most Excellent Masters; he invested them with power to travel into foreign countries in search of employment, and charged them to dispense light and truth to all uninformed brethren; but to those who chose to remain he furnished employment in keeping the temple in repair.

CHARGE

TO BE READ TO A MOST EXCELLENT MASTER AFTER HIS RECEPTION.

BROTHER—Your admittance to this degree of masonry is a proof of the good opinion the brethren of this lodge entertain of your masonic abilities. Let this consideration induce you to be careful of forfeiting, by misconduct and inattention to our rules, that esteem which has raised you to the rank you now possess.

It is one of your great duties as a Most Excellent Master, to dispense light and truth to the uninformed mason ; and I need not remind you of the impossibility of complying with this obligation, without possessing an accurate acquaintance with the lectures of each degree.

If you are not already completely conversant in all the degrees heretofore conferred on you, remember, that an indulgence, prompted by a belief that you will apply yourself with double diligence to make yourself so, has induced the brethren to accept you.

Let it therefore be your unremitting study to acquire such a degree of knowledge and information as shall enable you to discharge with propriety the various duties incumbent on you, and to preserve unsullied, the title now conferred upon you, of a MOST EXCELLENT MASTER.

CLOSING OF THE LODGE.

The following is read at closing:

Psalm xxiii.

"The Lord is my shepherd; I shall not want. He maketh me to lie down in green pastures; he leadeth me beside the still waters. He restoreth my soul; he leadeth me in the paths of righteousness for his name's sake. Yea, though I walk through the valley of the shadow of death, I will fear no evil; for thou art with me; thy rod and thy staff they comfort me. Thou preparest a table before me in the presence of mine enemies; thou anointest my head with oil; my cup runneth over. Surely goodness and mercy shall follow me all the days of my life; and I will dwell in the house of the Lord forever."

END OF THE MOST EXCELLENT MASTER'S DEGREE.

BOOK IV.

Royal Arch Mason.

"A degree indescribably more august, sublime and important than any which precede it; and is, in fact, the summit and perfection of ancient Masonry. It impresses on our minds a belief in the being of a God, without beginning of days or end of years, the great and incomprehensible Alpha and Omega, and reminds us of the reverence which is due to His holy NAME." '

OLIVER'S HISTORICAL LANDMARKS.

SEVENTH DEGREE.

SYMBOLICAL DESIGN.

In the preceding degrees we see the gradual progress of man from the cradle to the grave, depicted in his advancement through the several grades of the masonic system. We see him acquiring at his initiation the first elements of morality, and when about to represent the period of manhood, invested with new communications of a scientific character, and discharging the duties of life in various conditions. Again, at a later stage of his progress we find him attaining the experience of a well-spent life, and in the joyful hope of a blessed resurrection putting his house in order, and preparing for his final departure.

And now with reverential awe, we continue the sacred theme, and in the last degree symbolically allude to the rewards prepared for those who, in the pursuits of life, have distinguished themselves by a patient " continuance in well-doing."

Life, without some definite object in view, would be but a wearisome and monotonous existence. Every man, therefore, by the very instinct, as it were, of his nature, sets out with the proposed pursuit of some particular aim. To one it is wealth—to another, fame—to a third, pleasure. But whatever it may be, its attainment is considered as necessary to the happiness of the party seeking it.

The great object of pursuit in masonry—the scope and tendency of all its investigations—is TRUTH. This is the goal to which all masonic labor evidently tends. Sought for in every degree, and constantly approached, but never thoroughly and intimately embraced, at length, in the Royal Arch, the veils which concealed the object of search from our view are withdrawn, and the inestimable prize is revealed.

This truth which masonry makes the great object of its investigations, is not the mere truth of science, or the truth of history, but is the more important truth which is synonymous with the knowledge of the nature of God—that truth which is embraced in the sacred tetragrammaton or omnific name, including in its signification his eternal, present, past and future existence, and to which he himself alluded when he declared to Moses—"I appeared unto Abraham, unto Isaac, and unto Jacob, by the name of God Almighty: but by my name Jehovah was I not known unto them."

This knowledge of divine truth is never thoroughly attained in life; the corruptions of mortality, which encumber and cloud the human intellect, hide it as with a thick veil from mortal eyes. It is only beyond the tomb and when released from the burthen of life, that man is capable fully of receiving and appreciating the revelation. Hence, when we figuratively speak of its discovery in the Royal Arch degree, we mean to intimate that that sublime portion of the masonic system is a symbolic representation of the state after death. The vanities and follies of life are now supposed to be passed away— the first temple which we had erected with such consummate labor and apparent skill, for the reception of the Deity, has proved an imperfect and a transitory edifice; decay and desolation have fallen upon it, and from its ruins, deep beneath its foundations, and in the profound abyss of the grave, we find that mighty truth, in the search for which, life was spent in vain, and the mystic key to which death only could supply, when, having passed the portals of the grave, we shall begin to occupy that second temple, that house not made with hands, eternal in the heavens.

HISTORICAL SUMMARY.

Every reflecting mason must at once be struck with the fact that the third degree, or, as HUTCHINSON calls it, "The Master Mason's Order," presents all the appearance of being in a mutilated condition—that it is imperfect and unfinished in its history, and that, terminating abruptly as it does, it leaves the mind unsatisfied and craving for something that it does not and cannot supply. Now a reference to this fact is the first step towards an acquaintance with the true origin of the Royal Arch degree.

As an **independent** degree, given under a distinct jurisdiction and furnished with a separate but appropriate ritual, it is undoubtedly a modern degree, of comparatively recent establishment; but as a complement of the Master Mason's order, as supplying the deficiency of that degree in masonic symbolism it is, and of course must be, as old as the organization of which it forms so important and so necessary a part. The third degree is a symbolic memorial of events which took place at the first temple. The Royal Arch is equally a symbolic memorial of events that occurred at the second, and as the one would be incomplete without the other, we have every reason to suppose that each was adopted at the **earliest** period of the modern organization of Freemasonry as a memorial system. Indeed they must go together. The Royal Arch is the cape-stone of the masonic edifice, but the third degree is its foundation, and without the presence of both the building would be incomplete. The Royal Arch is absolutely necessary to the perfection of the Master's degree as a science of symbolism, and the latter cannot be understood without the developments of the former. They are the first and second volumes of a continuous history, and the absence of either would mutilate the work.

All of this, it must be remembered, is to be understood of the two degrees, simply in their modern organization, as a record, appropriated to a symbolic purpose, of the events to which they allude. Of course no one can indulge in the absurdity of supposing that the Royal Arch degree could have existed contemporaneously with the Master's at the time of the building of the first temple. Neither degree, in fact, in its present form is to be dated even at the later period of the building of the second. The events which they record of course occurred at the correct historic periods; but the organization and establishment of these degrees as records or memorials of these events, must have been a subsequent invention, when, we know not; nor is it essential to know. Certainly it was at a period beyond the memory of man, and outside of the records of history.

The Third Degree records a loss intrinsically of but little value, yet, in its symbolical reference, of the utmost importance. The Royal Arch records a recovery which is equally symbolical. The recovery cannot be appreciated unless we have first experienced the loss, and the loss would be unmeaning did we not subsequently meet with the recovery.

Accordingly, the Royal Arch degree was, anciently, always considered as a complement of the Master's, and was, therefore, originally conferred in symbolic lodges under the sanction of a Master's warrant. But as to the time when it was first dissevered from this connection and placed under a separate jurisdiction, masonic writers were not able to agree until the lucid explanations of the venerable Oliver* have completely settled the long vexed question.

* See "Some Account of the Schism which took place during the Last Century amongst the Free and Accepted Masons in England, showing the presumed Origin of the Royal Arch Degree," &c.

It seems to be evident, from the researches of this learned masonic historian, that until the year 1740, the essential element of the Royal Arch constituted a component part of the Master's degree, and was of course its concluding portion; that as a degree, it was not at all recognized, being but the complement of one; that about that time it was dissevered from its original connection and elevated to the position and invested with the form of a distinct degree by the body which called itself "the Grand Lodge of England according to the old Constitutions," but which is more familiarly known as the Dermott or the Atholl Grand Lodge, and frequently as "the ancients," in contradistinction to the legitimate Grand Lodge which was styled "the moderns."

The jurisdiction of the degree still however continued to be under Master's lodges, and many years elapsed before it was taken thence and placed under the control of distinct bodies called Grand Chapters. In America it was not until 1798 that a Grand Chapter was formed, and many lodges persisted for some years after in conferring the Royal Arch degree under the authority of their warrants from Grand Lodges.

5

OPENING OF THE CHAPTER.

A CHAPTER of Royal Arch Masons consists of the following twelve officers:

HIGH PRIEST.

KING.

SCRIBE.

CAPTAIN OF THE HOST.

PRINCIPAL SOJOURNER.

ROYAL ARCH CAPTAIN.

GRAND MASTER OF THE THIRD VEIL.

GRAND MASTER OF THE SECOND VEIL.

GRAND MASTER OF THE FIRST VEIL.

TREASURER.

SECRETARY.

SENTINEL.

The title of the High Priest is "Most Excellent." He represents Joshua, or Jeshua, who was the son of Josedech, and the High Priest of the Jews, when they returned from the Babylonian exile. He is seated in the east and clothed in the apparel of the ancient High Priest of the Jews. He wears a robe of blue, purple, scarlet and white linen, and is decorated with a breast-plate and mitre. On the front of the mitre is inscribed the words "HOLINESS TO THE LORD." His jewel is a mitre.

The King represents Zerubbabel, who was the son of Shealtiel, and the Prince of Judah, being lineally descended from King Solomon. He was the leader of the first colony of

Jews who returned from the captivity at Babylon to rebuild the city of Jerusalem and the temple of the Lord. He sits on the right hand of the High Priest, clothed in a scarlet robe, with a crown on his head and a sceptre in his hand. His jewel is a level surmounted by a crown.

The Scribe represents Haggai the prophet, who returned with Joshua and Zerubbabel to Jerusalem at the liberation of the Jews by Cyrus from their Babylonish captivity. He sits on the left hand of the High Priest clothed in a purple robe and wearing a turban of the same color. His jewel is a plumb-line surmounted by a turban. The *Sophar* or Scribe among the Jews at the period to which the Royal Arch degree refers, was a learned man whose duty it was to expound the law, and to take care of the records. He may be considered as in some measure a minister of state. Dr. Beard, in Kitto's Biblical Cyclopædia, thus describes the functions of the Scribes: "The Scribes had the care of the law; it was their duty to make transcripts of it; they also expounded its difficulties and taught its doctrines, and so performed several functions which are now distributed among different professions, being keepers of the records, consulting lawyers, authorized expounders of holy writ, and, finally, schoolmasters—thus blending together in one character the several elements of intellectual, moral, social, and religious influence. It scarcely needs to be added that their power was very great." These three officers constitute the Grand Council.

The Captain of the Host represents the general or leader of the Jewish troops who returned from Babylon and who was called "*Sar el hatzaba*," and was equivalent to a modern general. He sits on the right of the council in front, and wears a white robe, and cap or helmet with a red sash, and is armed with a sword. His jewel is a triangular plate, on which an armed soldier is engraved.

The Principal Sojourner represents the spokesman and leader of a small party of Israelites who had sojourned in Babylon for a short time after the departure of the main body of exiles, and subsequently came up to Jerusalem. He sits on the left of the council, in front, and wears a dark robe with a rose colored tesselated border, and a slouched hat and pilgrim's rod or staff. His jewel is a triangular plate, on which a pilgrim is engraved.

The Royal Arch Captain represents the "*sar hatabahim*" or Captain of the King's guards. He sits in front of the council and at the entrance of the fourth veil. He wears a white robe and cap, and is armed with a sword, and bears a white pennon or banner. His jewel is a sword.

The Grand Masters of the three veils represent the attendants on the tabernacle. They sit at the entrance of their respective veils, and wear robes and caps of different colors. The Master of the third veil wears a scarlet robe and cap, the Master of the second a purple robe and cap, and the Master of the first a blue robe and cap. Each is armed with a sword, and bears a flag or pennon of the same color as his robe and the veil which he guards. Their jewel is the same as that of the Royal Arch Captain.

The Treasurer, Secretary and Sentinel have no historical reference nor peculiar dress. The Treasurer wears as a jewel the cross keys, the Secretary the cross pens, and the Sentinel the cross swords.

The Jewels of a Chapter are of gold, and each is suspended within a triangle. Those of a Grand Chapter are suspended within a circle.

CLOTHING.

The symbolic color of this degree is scarlet.

The collar and sash of a Royal Arch Mason are scarlet, edged with gold. The sash passes from the left shoulder to the right hip; and on that part of it which crosses the breast, the words "HOLINESS TO THE LORD" should be painted or embroidered in gilt letters.

The apron is of white lamb-skin, edged with scarlet ribbon.

THE ROYAL ARCH EMBLEM.

The emblem of Royal Arch Masonry is the *triple tau* which is a figure of three tau crosses, conjoined after the following form:

The signification of this emblem has been variously interpreted. Some have supposed it to be the initials H. T. which may stand for *Hiram of Tyre*, or for *Templum Hierosolymæ*, the Temple of Jerusalem; and others, that it was intended to typify the sacred name of God. The following explanation is offered as the most probable one of the true meaning of this important emblem.

The *tau-cross*, **T** so called from its resemblance to the Greek letter *tau*, was among the ancients the hieroglyphic of eternal life. Among the Brahmins it was marked upon the bodies of candidates as a sign that they were set apart for initiation. It was also familiarly known to the Hebrews, and is thus alluded to in the vision of Ezekiel, (ix. 4,) "Go through the midst of the city and set a *tau* upon the foreheads of the men that sigh, and that cry for all the abominations that be done in the midst thereof." And this mark, or tau, was intended to distinguish those upon whom it was placed, as persons to be saved on account of their sorrow for sin, from those who as idolators were to be slain. The tau was therefore a symbol of those who were consecrated or set apart for some holy purpose. The triple tau may, with the same symbolic allusion, be supposed to be used in the Royal Arch degree, as designating and separating those who have been taught the true name of God, from those who are ignorant of that august mystery.

In English masonry, this emblem is so highly esteemed as to be styled the "emblem of all emblems," and the "grand emblem of Royal Arch Masonry." Within a triangle and circle it constitutes the Royal Arch jewel.* In America, this symbol has not been generally adopted; but at the triennial session of the General Grand Chapter of the United States, held at Chicago, in 1859, a Royal Arch apron was prescribed, consisting of a lamb-skin, (silk or satin being strictly prohibited,) to be lined and bound with scarlet; on the flap of which should be placed a triple tau, within a triangle and all within a circle.

Chapters of Royal Arch Masons are "dedicated to Prince Zerubbabel."

Candidates receiving this degree are said to be "exalted to the august degree of the Holy Royal Arch."

Documents connected with Royal Arch Masonry are dated from the era of the building of the second temple and the time of that important discovery which gave origin to the degree. Hence such documents are dated as A∴ I∴ that

---

* The English Royal Arch lectures thus define it. "The Triple Tau forms two right angles on each of the exterior lines, and another at the centre by their union; for the three angles of each triangle are equal to two right angles. This being triplified, illustrates the jewel worn by the companions of the Royal Arch; which by its intersection forms a given number of angles, that may be taken in five several combinations; and reduced, their amount in right angles will be found equal to the five Platonic bodies which represent the four elements and the sphere of the Universe."

is, *Anno Inventionis,* or, *in the Year of the discovery,* and as the second temple was begun to be built 530 before Christ, the Royal Arch date is found by adding 530 to the date of the Christian era. Thus the year 1858 would in **Royal Arch** documents be marked as A∴ I∴ 2388.

The following charge is read at the opening of a chapter:

II THESSALONIANS, iii. 6-16.

Now we command you, brethren, that ye withdraw yourselves from every brother that walketh disorderly, and not after the tradition which he received of us. For yourselves know how ye ought to follow us; for we behaved ourselves not disorderly among you. Neither did we eat any man's bread for nought, but wrought with labor and travail day and night that we might not be chargeable to any of you. Not because we have not power, but to make ourselves an ensample unto you to follow us. For even when we were with you, this we commanded you, that if any would not work, neither should he eat; for we hear there are some who walk among you disorderly, working not at all, but are busy-bodies. Now them that are such, we command and exhort, that with quietness they work, and eat their own bread. But ye, brethren, be not weary in well doing. And if any man obey not our word, note that man, and have no company with him, that he may be ashamed. Yet count him not as an enemy, but admonish him as a brother. Now the LORD of peace himself give you peace always.

The passage of Scripture here cited is an exhortation against idleness; and is very appropriately selected to be read at the opening of a chapter, to teach us that as Royal Arch Masons we are still called on to labor, freely and without weariness. Though the old temple be destroyed, we must labor in building the new; though the word be lost, we must labor for its recovery. Masonic labor is the search for the word — the search after Divine truth. This and this only is the mason's work, and the word is his reward.

Labor, said the old monks, is worship—"laborare est orare"—and thus in our sacred retreats do we worship—working for the truth—working for the word—ever looking forward—casting no glance behind—well knowing that, "if any will not work, neither shall he eat:" but cheerily hoping for the consummation and the reward of our labor in the sublime knowledge which is promised to him who plays no laggart's part; and which, when this earthly temple is dissolved, we shall find in that second temple, not made with hands, eternal in the heavens.

LECTURE AND RECEPTION.

The lecture in the Royal Arch degree is divided into two sections; and as Webb has very properly said, "It should be well understood by every Royal Arch Mason, as upon an accurate acquaintance with it will depend his usefulness at our assemblies, and without it he will be unqualified to perform the duties of the various stations in which his services may be required by the chapter." But beyond this assistance, which it gives in the practical working of the ceremonial of the degree, the lecture is of no utility. When the student desires light upon the history, the traditions and the symbolism of the Royal Arch, he must apply to other sources, and must make himself acquainted with the profane as well as sacred history of the times and events to which the degree refers, if he would thoroughly appreciate its esoteric teachings.

The following works, among others, are especially recommended to the perusal of the student in Royal Arch Masonry. They are all easily accessible :

" The Antiquities of the Jews," by Flavius Josephus ; the 9th, 10th and 11th books.

" The Old and New Testament connected in the History of the Jews and Neighboring Nations," by Humphrey Prideaux, D.D. Part I. Books 1, 2 and 3 are of essential use.

" A System of Speculative Masonry," by Rev. Salem Town, A.M. ; especially the 13th and 19th chapters.

" Some Account of the Schisms which took place during the last century amongst the Free and Accepted Masons in England, showing the Presumed Origin of the Royal Arch Degree ; by Rev. Geo. Oliver, D.D.

" The Insignia of the Royal Arch, as it was used at the first establishment of the degree, illustrated and explained ;" by the same author. These two works are always printed together; the one being supplementary to the other. Morris has republished them in the 13th volume of his Universal Masonic Library. They are highly interesting ; but no Royal Arch Mason can expect to be a thorough master of his science unless he attentively reads the following :

" The Historical Landmarks of Freemasonry," by Dr. Oliver; from the 33d to the 48th chapter. The 44th chapter on the tetragrammaton must be closely studied.

5*

FIRST SECTION OF THE LECTURE.

The first section explains the organization of a chapter, and the stations and duties of its officers. With this section every officer **of a** chapter **should be intimately ac-** quainted. A knowledge of it is essentially neccessary to all who are engaged in the ceremony of the opening of a chapter.

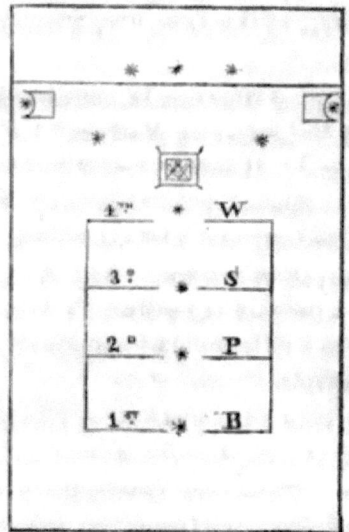

A Royal Arch Chapter *represents the tabernacle erected by* **our** *ancient brethren near the ruins of King Solomon's Temple.*

SYMBOLISM OF THE VEILS.

Blue, is emblematic of universal friendship and benevolence, and teaches us that those virtues should be as expansive in the breast of every mason as the blue vault of heaven itself.

Purple, being formed by a due admixture of blue and scarlet, is intended to remind us of the intimate connection that exists between symbolic masonry and the Royal Arch degree.

Scarlet, is emblematic of that fervency and zeal which should actuate all Royal Arch Masons, and is peculiarly characteristic of this degree.

White, is emblematic of that purity of life and rectitude of conduct by which alone we can expect to gain admission into the holy of holies above.

SECOND SECTION.

The Second Section of the Royal Arch Lecture furnishes valuable information in reference to the events that are commemorated in this degree, and correctly details the ceremony of exaltation. It may, for convenience, be appropriately divided into two clauses, each referring to a different historic period.

FIRST CLAUSE.

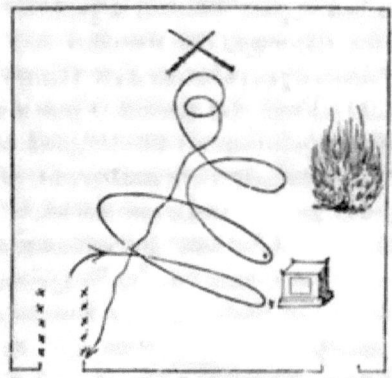

Our attention is here invited by appropriate symbolic ceremonies to the destruction of the city of Jerusalem, and the temple of the Lord by the Chaldean monarch Nebuchadnezzar, who carried the Jews as captives into Babylon.

The following passages of Scripture are to be recited during this clause of the ceremony of exaltation :

ISAIAH xlii. 16.

I will bring the blind by a way that they knew
not ; I will lead them in paths that they have not
known ; I will make darkness light before them,
and crooked things straight : these things will I do
unto them and not forsake them.

As the return of the captives from Babylon forms a promi-
nent reference in the Royal Arch degree, it was exceedingly
appropriate to commence the ritual by a selection of these
words from Isaiah, which form a part of that series of sublime chapters in which, as Bishop Lowth remarks, "the return of the Jews from the captivity of Babylon is the first,
though not the principal thing in the prophet's view."
These verses, in particular, contain a promise of guidance
and protection to the captives through the uncultivated
deserts and barbarous people that were interposed between
Babylon and Jerusalem. Of course it has a sublimer prophetic sense, which the pious and intelligent candidate will
readily apply. Masonically it is analogous to a similar encouragement given in the commencement of the Entered
Apprentice's degree to him who puts his trust in God. It
is well, on all such occasions, in the incipiency of his masonic journey to remind the candidate that *he is in the hands
of a true and trusty friend in whom he may well confide,*
which friend is none other than the G A O T U.

*   *

*   *

*   *

*   *

*   *

*   *

The Divine Master has said, "he that humbleth himself shall be exalted," (Luke xxiii. 11 ;) and thus after being first taught to put his trust in God as a faithful friend and guide, the recipient next learns by an impressive ceremony the necessity of humiliation and self-abasement. Humility is an essential virtue to all who are engaged in the search after truth. Plato says, that truth lies concealed in a well, which thought may perhaps be intended to teach us that we should look for it in the humblest places. Humility is a virtue carefully inculcated throughout the Sacred Scriptures, as ever meeting its reward in subsequent exaltation. It is with diffidence and humility that the wise man should approach such mysterious subjects as the nature and attributes of Deity. The mason who seeks advancement must lay aside all pride and arrogance, and with an humble spirit, a readiness to learn, and an anxiety to be taught, must throw himself at the feet of his preceptor and receive the new light and truth for which he craves. And so the candidate for the sublime mysteries of this august degree is first to learn on its very threshold to bow his head and to stoop low, ever remembering that, he that humbleth himself shall be exalted.

During the ceremony of exaltation, it is proper to recite the following

PRAYER.

Supreme Architect of the Universe, who, by thine Almighty Word, didst speak into being the stupendous arch of heaven, and for the instruction and pleasure of thy rational creatures, didst adorn us with greater and lesser lights, thereby magnifying thy power, and endearing thy goodness unto the sons of men : We humbly adore and worship thine unspeakable perfection. We bless thee, that when man had fallen from his innocence and happiness, thou didst leave him the powers of reasoning, and capacity of improvement and of pleasure. We thank thee that amidst the pains and calamities of our present state, so many means of refreshment and satisfaction are reserved to us, while traveling the *rugged path* of life ; especially would we, at this time, render thee our thanksgiving and praise for the institution, as members of which we are at this time, assembled, and for all the pleasures we have **derived** from it. We thank thee that the few here assembled before thee, have been favored with new inducements, and been laid under new and stronger obligations of virtue and holiness. May these obligations, O blessed Father! have their full effect upon us. Teach us, we pray thee, the true reverence of thy great, **mighty,** and terrible name. Inspire us with a firm and **unshaken** resolution in **our** virtuous pursuits. Give us grace diligently to search thy word in the book of nature, wherein the duties of our high vocation are inculcated with divine authority.

May the solemnity of the ceremonies of our institution be duly impressed on our minds, and have a happy and lasting effect on our lives! O thou, who didst aforetime appear unto thy servant Moses *in a flame of fire out of the midst of a bush*, enkindle, we beseech thee, in each of our hearts, a flame of devotion to thee, of love to each other, and of charity to all mankind! May all thy miracles and mighty works fill us with thy dread, and thy goodness impress us with a love of thy holy name! May *Holiness to the Lord*, be engraven upon all our thoughts, words, and actions! May the incense of piety ascend continually unto thee, from the altar of our hearts and burn day and night, as a sacrifice of sweet smelling savor, well pleasing unto thee! And since sin has destroyed within us the first temple of purity and innocence, may thy heavenly grace guide and assist us in rebuilding a *second temple* of reformation, and may the glory of this latter house, be greater than the glory of the former! So mote it be. Amen.

" The fraternity," says Bro. SCOTT,* are taught the necessity of appealing to the throne of heaven before entering upon any important undertaking. To the Father of all we must ask for strength and power to support us in every trial, duty, and emergency in life. It is not difficult for us to learn who taught us to pray, and how to pray. The

* Analogy of Anc. Craft Masonry, p. 33.

Holy One prompts the sinful heart to plead for forgiveness, and ask for heavenly things."

Kneeling is the appropriate attitude in which this sublime prayer should be offered up. "Kneeling," says HORNE,* " was ever considered to be the proper posture of supplication, as it expressed humility, contrition, and subjection. For as among the ancients, the forehead was consecrated to genius, the ear to memory, and the right hand to faith, so the knees were consecrated to mercy."

The extended duties and obligations of this degree are next referred to by those impressive ceremonies which are peculiar to Freemasonry.   The obligations imposed by exaltation to this august degree, although of the most solemn nature, are still eminently practical in their nature, for it must be remembered, to borrow the language of a distinguished brother,† that as " the order of masonry was instituted for the improvement of mankind, so it demands the performance of no duty, the practice of no principle that is extravagant or impracticable."

* Intro. to Crit. Study and Knowl. of the Holy Script. v. ii., part iii., ch. v., sect. ii., p. 131.   † Albert Pike.

EXODUS iii. 1–6.

Now Moses kept the flock of Jethro his father-in-law, the priest of Midian ; and he led the flock to

the back side of the desert, and came to the mountain of God, even to Horeb.   And the angel of the
LORD appeared unto him in a flame of fire out of the
midst of a bush, and he looked, and, behold the bush
burned with fire, and the bush was not consumed.

And when the LORD saw that he turned aside to
see, GOD called to him out of the bush and said,
Moses, Moses!   And he said, Here am I.   And he
said, Draw not nigh hither : put off thy shoes from
off thy feet, for the place whereon thou standest is
holy ground.   Moreover he said, I am the GOD of
thy father, the GOD of Abraham, the GOD of Isaac,
and the GOD of Jacob.   And Moses hid his face, for
he was afraid to look upon GOD.

* * *

THE BURNING BUSH.

It was at the Burning Bush that Moses received that divine commission in fulfillment of which he composed the
Pentateuch.   And as it is from these writings of Moses
that we derive all those significant teachings by which a
Royal Arch Mason is eminently distinguished from the rest
of the fraternity, it is peculiarly appropriate to introduce
the instructions, hereafter to be given, by a recital of the
passage which details the circumstances under which the
Jewish lawgiver received the power and authority to perform those miracles which are referred to in subsequent
parts of the degree.

But the Burning Bush, as the spot where the G. A. O. T. U.
first made himself known to Moses, and through him to his
chosen people, becomes to the Royal Arch Mason, the source

of light and knowledge, and takes the position occupied by the *East* in symbolic masonry. And hence, in some of the higher degrees, masonic documents are dated not from "the East" but from the "B∴ B∴" that is, the Burning Bush.

The following passages of Scripture are read with impressive ceremonies:

II. CHRONICLES, xxxvi. 11–20.

Zedekiah was one-and-twenty years old when he began to reign, and reigned eleven years in Jerusalem. And he did that which was evil in the sight of the LORD his GOD, and humbled not himself before Jeremiah the prophet speaking from the mouth of the LORD. And he also rebelled against king Nebuchadnezzar; but he stiffened his neck, and hardened his heart, from turning unto the LORD GOD of Israel. Moreover, all the chief of the priests, and the people, transgressed very much after all the abominations of the heathen; and polluted the house of the LORD, which he had hallowed in Jerusalem. And the LORD GOD of their fathers sent to them by his messengers, rising up betimes and sending; because he had compassion on his people, and on his dwelling place. But they mocked the messengers of GOD, and des-

pised his words, and misused his prophets, until the
wrath of the LORD arose against his people, till there
was no remedy. Therefore he brought upon them the
king of the Chaldees, who slew their young men with
the sword in the house of their sanctuary, and had
no compassion on young man or maiden, old man,
or him that stooped for age ; he gave them all into
his hand. And all the vessels of the house of GOD,
great and small, and the treasures of the house of
the LORD, and treasures of the king, and of his
princes ; all these he brought to Babylon.   And
they burnt the house of GOD, and brake down the
wall of Jerusalem, and burnt all the palaces thereof
with fire, and destroyed all the goodly vessels thereof. And them that had escaped from the sword carried he away to Babylon; where they were servants
to him and his sons, until the reign of the kingdom
of Persia.

THE DESTRUCTION OF JERUSALEM.

The Temple was destroyed in the year of the world 3416
and 588 years before the birth of Christ, being just 416
years since its dedication by King Solomon. For a more
particular detail of the events connected with the destruction of the temple, the reader is referred to the first lecture
on the Royal Arch history appended to this book.

With the destruction of the temple and the city of Jerusalem and the carrying of the Jews into captivity, ends the
first clause of the Royal Arch reception.

SECOND CLAUSE.

The second clause commences by a reference to that happy period when Cyrus, having overthrown the Chaldean dynasty, restored the captive Jews to liberty and permitted them to return to Jerusalem for the purpose of rebuilding the house of the Lord.

The ceremonies begin by a recital of the following passages of Scripture:

C∴ H∴

Now in the first year of Cyrus, king of Persia, the Lord stirred up the spirit of Cyrus, king of Persia, that he made a proclamation throughout all his kingdom, and put it also in writing, saying: Thus saith Cyrus, king of Persia, the Lord God of heaven hath given me all the kingdoms of the earth, and he hath charged me to build him an house at Jerusalem, which is in Judah. Who is there among you of all his people? his God be with him, and let him go up to Jerusalem, which is in Judah, and build the house of the Lord God of Israel, which is in Jerusalem.*

* Ezra i. 1–3.

P∴ S∴

And Moses said unto God, Behold! when I come
unto the children of Israel, and shall say unto them,
the God of your fathers hath sent me unto you, and
they shall say to me, What is his name? What shall
I say to them?*

C∴ H∴

And God said unto Moses, I AM THAT I AM: And
thus shalt thou say unto the children of Israel, I AM
hath sent me unto you.†

The Egyptians worshipped the Sun as their chief deity,
under the appellation of ON, and it was to distinguish himself as the true and only God that Jehovah in the passage
just recited instructed Moses to inform the Iraelites that he
came to them by the authority of him who was I AM THAT
I AM, which term signifies the *Self Existent Being*. This
method of denoting the Supreme Deity was adopted by the
Jews under the teachings of Moses, and distinguished them
from all heathen nations of the world. It became, therefore,
the shibboleth, as it were, of their religion, and was appropriately selected as a token by which the captives might on
their arrival at Jerusalem, prove themselves to be the true
children of the covenant and worthy to be employed in the
task of rebuilding the house of the Lord.

THE RETURN OF THE JEWS FROM THE CAPTIVITY.

The return of the captives from Babylon to Jerusalem
through a barren wilderness beset by hostile tribes and over
a dry desert unsupplied with water to quench their thirst, or

---

* Exodus iii. 13.   † Exodus iii. 14.

any means of subsistence, must have proved to these weary and footsore pilgrims a *rough and rugged road.* The passages of Scripture selected as a memorial of the tribulations of that journey are appropriately taken from those Psalms which are supposed to have been written by David when in circumstances of great distress—the first when he was flying from the anger of Saul; the second when concealed in the cave of En-gedi from the persecutions of his enemies; and the last, when in great sorrow on account of the rebellion of his son Absalom. They are here, however, referred, as they have been by some commentators, to the condition of the exiles at Babylon.

Psalm, cxli.

Lord, I cry unto thee : make haste unto me ; give ear unto my voice. Let my prayer be set forth before thee, as incense : and the lifting up of my hands as the evening sacrifice. Set a watch, O Lord, before my mouth ; keep the door of my lips. Incline not my heart to any evil thing, to practice wicked works with men that work iniquity. Let the righteous smite me ; it shall be a kindness : and let him reprove me ; it shall be an excellent oil. Mine eyes are unto thee, O God the Lord ; in thee is my trust ; leave not my soul destitute. Keep me from the snare which they have laid for me, and the gins of the workers of iniquity. Let the wicked fall into their own nets, whilst that I withal escape.

* * * * * *

* * * * * *

PSALM cxlii.

I cried unto the LORD with my voice ; with my voice unto the Lord did I make my supplication. I poured out my complaint before him ; I showed before him my trouble. When my spirit was overwhelmed within me, then thou knewest my path. In the way wherein I walked, have they privily laid a snare for me. I looked on my right hand, and beheld, but there was no man that would know me ; refuge failed me : no man cared for my soul. I cried unto thee, O LORD ; I said, Thou art my refuge and my portion in the land of the living. Attend unto my cry, for I am brought very low ; deliver me from my persecutors ; for they are stronger than I. Bring my soul out of prison, that I may praise thy name.

Psalm clxiii.

Hear my prayer, O Lord ; give ear to my supplications : in thy faithfulness answer me, and in thy righteousness. And enter not into judgment with thy servant : for in thy sight shall no man living be justified.

For the enemy hath persecuted my soul ; he hath made me to dwell in darkness. Therefore is my spirit overwhelmed within me ; my heart within me is desolate. Hear me speedily, O Lord : my spirit faileth : hide not thy face from me, lest I be like unto them that go down into the pit. Cause me to hear thy loving kindness in the morning ; for in thee do I trust : cause me to know the way wherein I should walk, for I lift up my soul unto thee. Bring my soul out of trouble, and of thy mercy cut off mine enemies : for I am thy servant.

But rough and rugged as was the road, and long and toilsome as was the march, it at last came to an end, and the weary sojourners were blessed with a sight of the ruined walls of Jerusalem and the glistening tents of their brethren. Here they turned aside to rest ; and here too we may pause in our review of the ritual, to investigate the nature of the temporary tabernacle which is said to have been erected by the Jewish leaders near the ruins of the temple.

THE TABERNACLE.

We are not to suppose that the tabernacle represented in the ceremonies of the Royal Arch degree is an exact copy of the tabernacle constructed by Moses, and which served as a pattern for that erected by Zerubbabel and his colleagues near the ruins of King Solomon's Temple. It is unnecessary here to enter into an elaborate description of the Mosaic tabernacle; it will be sufficient to say that although the colors of the veils were the same, namely, blue, purple, scarlet, and fine linen, yet their disposition was entirely different from that observed in the tabernacle of the Royal Arch.

This is, however, a matter of not the slightest importance to the substantial character and design of the degree. The tabernacle erected by Zerubbabel and the restored captives was intended for practical purposes of religious observance, and was obliged to be constructed according to the exact specifications laid down in the twenty-sixth chapter of Exodus. The tabernacle used in Freemasonry is altogether symbolical, and therefore architectural correctness was by no means necessary to the preservation of the symbols inculcated by it.

It is the same thing in respect to the analogy of the blue lodge to Solomon's temple. The former is a representation of the latter, only in a symbolic sense. And yet a great superfluity of learning has been wasted by some writers to prove that the whole system of Freemasonry is a failure, simply because the position, the form and decorations of the temple are not accurately preserved in every village lodge room throughout the country. For instance, Dr. Dalcho, in his "Orations," thinks he discovers an insurmountable error in the ritual of the Master's degree, because in the ancient temple "there *was* a gate on the *north* side, but *none* on the *west*, because the Sanctum Sanctorum was built there." Dalcho, in this passage, as well as in many others of the same work, and in the notes to his Ahiman Rezon, shows very conclusively that he was not intimately conversant with the esoteric symbolism of the order. It is essential to the symbolic instruction of Masonry, that there should be a gate on the west and none on the north of the lodge, but it by no means affects the integrity of our system that a different arrangement existed at the temple. We *must* preserve the symbolism, but we *may* neglect the architectural details.

So in the Masonic tabernacle, the four colors of the veils in the Mosaic tabernacle have been preserved because these colors are symbolic; but no attention has been paid to their correct distribution, as in this there was no symbolism.

We say then, with these explanatory remarks, that in the Royal Arch degree, we represent the tabernacle erected by our ancient brethren near the ruins of King Solomon's temple.

PRIDEAUX denies that any such tabernacle was erected by the captives on their return; but Bishop Patrick, an almost equally learned authority, thinks that there was; and says, in his Commentary on 1 Chron. ix. 11, "As before the first temple was built there was a tabernacle for divine service, so after the second was founded, they erected a tabernacle till this temple could be finished. Without which they could not have performed the several parts of the worship of God which were annexed to the several parts of the holy places, according to law."

Reason, as well as masonic tradition, support the opinion of Bishop Patrick.

THE SIGNS OF MOSES.

The reference in a previous part of the degree to the Burning Bush, where God first made his true name known to Moses, has prepared the mind for the reception of those other revelations of the divine interview, in which the Deity communicated to the patriarch those miraculous signs by which he was to convince the people to whom he was to be sent of the truth of his mission. And hence we now begin to recite from the books of Moses the account of the establishment of these signs. The symbolism is here worthy of attention. As these signs were ordained by their divine author to establish the authority of the mission in which the Jewish lawgiver was to be engaged in rescuing his people from the darkness of Egyptian idolatry, and in bringing them to the knowledge and worship of the true God, so are they here symbolic of the evidence which every mason is to give of his mission in rescuing himself from the bondage of falsehood and in searching for divine truth

Exodus iv. 1—5.

And Moses answered and said, But behold, they will not believe me, nor hearken unto my voice : for they will say, The Lord hath not appeared unto thee. And the Lord said unto him, What is that in thine hand ? And he said, A rod. And he said, Cast it on the ground : and he cast it on the ground, and it became a serpent ; and Moses fled from before it. And the Lord said unto Moses, Put forth thine hand, and take it by the tail. And he put forth his hand and caught it, and it became a rod in his hand. That they may believe that the Lord God of their fathers, the God of Abraham, the God of Isaac, and the God of Jacob, hath appeared unto thee.

The serpent has always been considered by masonic writers as a legitimate symbol of Freemasonry, and yet it is singular that in the whole ritual of the York rite this is the only instance in which any allusion is made to it. In the other masonic systems it is, however, repeatedly referred to. Dr. Oliver says that, " amongst masons it serves to remind us of our fall in Adam and our restoration in Christ." These events are symbolically represented in masonry by the loss and recovery of the word. Hence the reference in this place to the symbol of the serpent must in this view be considered as peculiarly appropriate.

In the course of these ceremonies reference is made at different times, to three important constructions in Scriptural history, namely, the three arks and the three tabernacles.

Here our attention is invited by memorial words to the first ark, the ark of safety, which was constructed by *Shem*, *Ham* and *Japhet*, under the superintendence of **Noah**, and in which, as a tabernacle of refuge, the chosen family took temporary shelter until the subsidence of the waters of the deluge.*

EXODUS vi. 4–8.

And the Lord said furthermore unto him, Put now thine hand into thy bosom; and he put his hand into his bosom; and when he took it out, behold, his hand was leprous as snow. And he said, Put thine hand into thy bosom again; and he put his hand into his bosom again; and he plucked it out of his bosom, and, behold, it was turned again as his other flesh. And it shall come to pass, if they will not believe

* That the ark of Noah was also a tabernacle of Jehovah is the opinion of many learned biblical commentators. Dr. Jarvis, speaking of the *zohar*, which in our common version of Genesis vi. 16, has been translated "window," says, "I take it to have been the Divine Shechinah or glory of Jehovah, dwelling between the cherubim, which were now brought from their place at the east of Eden, as the ark afterwards was from the Holy of Holies of the Tabernacle into the Holy of Holies of the first Temple."—*Church of the Redeemed.* *Vol.* 1, *p.* 20, *note* 8.

thee, neither hearken to the voice of the first sign, that they will believe the voice of the latter sign.

Here, again, in the hand becoming leprous and being then restored to soundness, we have a repetition of the reference to the loss and the recovery of the word; the word itself being but a symbol of divine truth, the search for which constitutes the whole science of Freemasonry, and the symbolism of which pervades the whole system of initiation from the first to the last degree.

And here we have an allusion to the second ark and tabernacle, the ark of the covenant and the tabernacle in the wilderness, which were constructed by *Moses*, *Aholiab* and *Bezaleel*, as we find recorded in Exodus xxxvi. 2, "And Moses called Bezaleel and Aholiab, and every wise-hearted man in whose heart the Lord had put wisdom, even every one whose heart stirred him up, to come unto the work to do it." And in a previous passage (xxxi. 1–7), "And the Lord spake unto Moses, saying, See, I have called by name Bezaleel, the son of Uri, the son of Hur, of the tribe of Judah, and I have filled him with the Spirit of God in wisdom, and in understanding, and in knowledge, and in all manner of workmanship, to devise cunning works, to work in gold, and in silver, and in brass, and in cutting of stones to set them, and in carving of timber, to work in all manner of workmanship. And I, behold, I have given with him Aholiab, the son of Ahisamach, of the tribe of Dan, and in the hearts of all that are wise-hearted I have put wisdom that they may make all that I have commanded thee: the tabernacle of the congregation, and the ark of the testimony, and the mercy seat that is thereupon, and all the furniture of the tabernacle."*

* The reference at this place which is made in some chapters to Adoniram, who was one of the craftsmen at the temple of Solomon, and the mixture of his name with that of two of the sons of Noah who lived almost two thousand years before him, is so preposterous an anachronism, as to prove that it is a palpable innovation, at first introduced by some ignorant ritualist, and per-

EXODUS iv. 9.

And it shall come to pass, if they will not believe also these two signs, neither hearken unto thy voice, that thou shalt take of the water of the river, and pour it upon the dry land : and the water which thou takest out of the river, shall become blood upon the dry land.

The last miraculous sign by which Moses was to establish his authority and to prove his mission among the Jews and the Egyptians is here recited. Masonically it bears the same symbolic reference as the other two, to a change for the better —from a lower to a higher state—from the elemental water in which there is no life, to the blood which is the life itself— from darkness to light. The progress is still onward to the recovery of that which had been lost, but which is yet to be found.

And here we find an allusion to the tabernacle erected for temporary worship by *Joshua, Haggai* and *Zerubbabel,* and to that imitative ark for whose history we are traditionally said to be indebted to the exertions of those illustrious personages.

petuated by subsequent carelessness. It cannot be explained on any principles of symbolism; it is supported by none of the writers on Royal Arch Masonry, all of whom here make the reference to the constructors of the tabernacle and ark of the testimony; and it is absurd and nonsensical, and therefore manifestly not masonic. These three rules—the fitness of symbolism, the allusions and authority of learned writers, and the absence of absurdity, are excellent ones for judging in all disputed questions of ritualism where the nature of oral tradition deprives us of any others more direct.

The *signet of Zerubbabel,* which is adopted as one of the Royal Arch symbols, will be explained after the recital of the passage of Scripture which refers to it.

HAGGAI ii. 2-8.

In that day, saith the Lord of hosts, will I take thee, O Zerubbabel, my servant, the son of Shealtiel, saith the Lord, and will make thee as a signet: for I have chosen thee, saith the Lord of hosts.

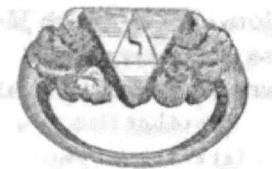

THE SIGNET OF ZERUBBABEL.

The signet of Zerubbabel, or, as it is more properly explained, the *signet of truth,* is in this place a symbol of the promise that the search of the neophyte for truth will now speedily meet with its reward. The signet, or private seal, most frequently in the form of a signet ring, was anciently often given by monarchs, or other persons of high condition, instead of a written testimonial, to their servants as a token of some authority which had been delegated, and of which the possession of the signet was, therefore, the only evidence. Haggai, who came to Jerusalem to excite the Jews to greater diligence in the work of rebuilding the temple, thus encouraged them by the declaration that the Lord had made their leader, Zerubbabel, his signet. He had exalted him, to use the language of Dr. CLARKE, "to high dignity, power and trust, of which the signet was the instrument, or sign, in those days." He was to be under God's peculiar care, and to be to him very precious, and thus the signet of truth is presented to the aspirant to assure him that he is advancing in his progress to the attainment of truth, and that he is thus invested with the power to pursue the search. He who has got thus far in Royal Arch Masonry becomes the sworn servant of truth, and the signet is the token of his elevation.

As to the form of the signet, which in many chapters is most improperly represented by a triangular plate of metal, it may be observed that it always was a finger ring with some device upon it, and it is so called because it was anciently used, as it still is in the East, for the purpose of enabling the wearer to seal with it important documents, instead of subscribing his name, which, it is well known, that even royal personages, in early times, were often unable to do, from their ignorance of the art of writing.

These signets, or seal rings, called by the Hebrews *chotam*, are repeatedly alluded to in Scripture. They appear to have been known and used at an early period; for we find that when JUDAH asks TAMAR what pledge he shall give her, she replies, "Thy signet, and thy bracelets, and thy staff that is in thine hand."—Gen. xxxviii. 18. They were worn on the finger, generally the index finger, and always on the right hand, as being the most honorable; thus in Jeremiah (xxii. 24.) we read: "as I live, saith the LORD, though Coniah, the son of Jehoiakim, king of Judah, were the signet upon my right hand, yet would I pluck thee thence." They were also inscribed with some appropriate device by which the owner might be identified. The art of doing this must have been well known even in the days of Moses, for we find an allusion to engraving on stone, "like the engravings of a signet," in the directions for making the breast-plate, as laid down in Exodus xxviii. 11.

6*

What was the particular device inscribed on the signet ring of ZERUBBABEL we cannot now determine, but we may conjecture, and perhaps approximate to truth. The signets of the ancients were generally sculptured with religious symbols, or the heads of their deities. The sphynx and the sacred beetle were favorite signets among the Egyptians. The former was adopted from that people by the Roman Emperor AUGUSTUS. The Babylonians followed the same custom, and many of their signets, remaining to this day, exhibit beautifully sculptured images of BAAL-BERITH, and other Chaldean deities. It was, perhaps, from the Babylonians that ZERUBBABEL learned the practice of wearing one, for HERODOTUS tells us that every Babylonian had a signet.

But the anti-idolatrous character of his faith must have prevented the Jewish prince from using any of the Chaldean objects of worship as a seal. May he not rather have adopted the great religious symbol of the Hebrews, and inscribed upon his signet ring the tetragrammaton or omnific name? Whether he did or not, this would at least be a most appropriate representation in our chapters of the seal of the illustrious builder of the second temple.

Incense burns day and night on the altar of the Lord.

The burning of incense constituted an essential part of the service of the temple, and large quantities of it were offered twice a day, at the morning and the evening sacrifice.

Impostors among the Workmen.

The following passage of Scripture from the 4th chapter of Ezra, verses 1 to 5, although forming no part of the ritual, may be read for a better understanding of the condition of affairs commemorated in this degree.

"Now when the adversaries of Judah and Benjamin heard that the children of the captivity builded the temple unto the Lord God of Israel; then they came to Zerubbabel, and to the chief of the fathers, and said unto them, Let us build with you: for we seek your God as ye do; and we do sacrifice unto him since the days of Esar-haddon, king of Assur, which brought us up hither. But Zerubbabel and Joshua, and the rest of the chiefs of the fathers of Israel, said unto them, Ye have nothing to do with us to build a house unto our God, but we ourselves together will build unto the Lord God of Israel, as king Cyrus the king of Persia has commanded us. Then the people of the land weakened the hands of the people of Judah, and troubled them in building; and hired counsellors against them, to frustrate their purpose, all the days of Cyrus king of Persia, even unto the reign of Darius king of Persia."

The exclusive character of the Jewish religion, separated as it always had been, by peculiar rites and a more exalted doctrine from that of every surrounding nation, made it impossible for its disciples to permit those who were not of the true and ancient faith to unite with them in any holy or religious work. Hence the builders of the second temple were extremely vigilant in seeing that no "impostors" from among "the adversaries," that is, the Samaritans and the other nations with which the kings of Assyria had peopled Israel, should be allowed to mingle with the workmen. All who came up to this sacred task were bound to afford the evidence that they were *the descendants of those faithful Giblemites who had wrought at the building of the first temple, who at its completion and dedication were received and acknowledged as Most Excellent Masters, at its destruction by Nebuchadnezzar were carried captives into Babylon, and being released by the proclamation of Cyrus, king of Persia, had come up to assist in the glorious task of rebuilding the house of the Lord without the hope of fee or reward.* These, and these alone were permitted to engage in the construction of the edifice.

WORKING TOOLS.

The working tools of a Royal Arch Mason are sometimes explained as follows:

The working tools of a Royal Arch Mason are the *Crow, Pick-axe* and *Spade.* The *Crow* is used by operative masons to raise things of great weight and bulk; the *Pick-axe* to loosen the soil and prepare it for digging; and the *Spade* to remove rubbish. But the Royal Arch Mason is emblematically taught to use them for more noble purposes. By them he is reminded that it is his sacred duty to lift from his mind the heavy weight of passions and prejudices which encumber his progress towards virtue, loosening the hold which long habits of sin and folly have had upon his disposition, and removing the rubbish of vice and ignorance, which prevents him

from beholding that eternal foundation of truth and
wisdom upon which he is to erect the spiritual and
moral temple of his second life.

THE KEYSTONE.

Until within a few years, architectural authorities have
denied the antiquity of the arch and keystone, and have
attributed their invention to a period not anterior to the
era of the Roman emperor Augustus. Such a theory, if correct, would of course invalidate the historical truth of an
important portion of the Royal Arch degree. Fortunately,
therefore, the researches of modern archæologists have
traced the existence of the arch as far back as five hundred
and fifty years before the building of King Solomon's temple,
and thus completely reconciled the traditions of Freemasonry with the accuracy of history.

Mr. WILKINSON, the great Egyptian traveler, says that the
arch " was evidently used in the tombs of the Egyptians as
early as the commencement of the eighteenth dynasty, or
about 1540 B.C.; and judging from some of the drawings at
Beni Hassan, it seems to have been known in the time of
the first OSIRTASEN, whom I suppose to have been contemporary with JOSEPH." *

* Manners and Customs of Anc. Egyptians, vol. ii. p. 117.

"After this," says KITTO, "it seems unreasonable to doubt that the arch was known to the Hebrews also, and employed in their buildings."

But in the decision of the question we are not left to the suggestions of probability. Portions of the immense substructions of the temple of Solomon still exist, and have been recently discovered and explored. Messrs. SCOLES and CATHERWOOD, two English architects, were the first to notice the commencement of the spandril of an arch springing from these subterranean works towards Mount Zion, and Dr. JARVIS suggests that this arch "may have been part of the construction of Solomon's private entrance into the temple."* The researches of subsequent travelers have discovered other vaults and arches beneath the temple, evidently the work of SOLOMON.

Freemasonry is throughout so connected a system that we are continually meeting in an inferior degree with something that is left to be explained in a higher. Such is the case with *the three squares of our ancient Grand Masters*, whose peculiar history can only be understood by those who have advanced to the degree of Select Master.

The following quotation from the learned Dr. Lightfoot's "Prospect of the Temple," (ch. 15,) will at this time be read with interest by the Royal Arch Mason:

* Church of the Redeemer, vol. 1. p. 258.

"It is fancied by the Jews, that Solomon, when he built the temple, foreseeing that the temple should be destroyed, caused very obscure and intricate vaults under ground to be made, wherein to hide the ark when any such danger came; that howsoever it went with the temple, yet the ark, which was the very life of the temple, might be saved. And they understand that passage in II Chron. xxxv. 3, ' Josiah said unto the Levites, put the holy ark into the house which Solomon, the son of David, did build,' &c., as if Josiah, having heard by the reading of Moses' manuscript and by Huldah's prophecy of the danger that hung over Jerusalem,—commanded to convey the ark into this vault, that it might be secured; and with it, say they, they laid up Aaron's rod, the pot of manna, and the anointing oil. For while the ark stood in its place, upon the stone mentioned,—they hold that Aaron's rod and the pot of manna stood before it; but, now, were all conveyed into obscurity—and the stone upon which the ark stood lay over the mouth of the vault. But Rabbi Solomon, which useth not, ordinarily, to forsake such traditions, hath given a more serious gloss upon the place; namely, that whereas Manasseh and Amon had removed the ark out of its habitation, and set up images and abominations there of their own,—Joshua speaketh to the priests to restore it to its place again. What became of the ark, at the burning of the temple by Nebuchadnezzar, we read not; it is most likely, it went to the fire also. However it sped, it was not in the second temple; and is one of the five choice things that the Jews reckon wanting there. Yet they had an ark there also of their own making, as they had a breast-plate of judgment; which, though they both wanted the glory of the former, which was giving of oracles, yet did they stand current as to the other matters of their worship, as the former breast-plate and ark had done."

The idea of the concealment of an ark and its accompanying treasures always prevailed in the Jewish church. The account given by the talmudists is undoubtedly mythical, but there must, as certainly, have been some foundation for the myth, for every myth has a substratum of truth. The masonic tradition differs from the rabbinical, but is in every way more reconcilable with truth, or at least with probability. The ark constructed by Moses, Aholiab and Bezaleel was burnt at the destruction of the first temple—but there was an exact representation of it in the second, of whose origin Royal Arch Masonry alone gives an account.

The Book of the Law—Long lost but now found.

The Book of the Law furnishes us with the following passages, which may be appropriately read.

Genesis i. 1–3.

In the beginning God created the heavens and the earth. And the earth was without form, and void ; and darkness was upon the face of the deep ; and the Spirit of God moved upon the face of the waters. And God said, Let there be light : and there was light.

Deuteronomy xxxi. 24–26.

And it came to pass, when Moses had made an end of writing the words of this law in a book, until they were finished, that Moses commanded the Levites which bare the ark of the covenant of the Lord, saying, Take this book of the law, and put it in the side of the ark of the covenant of the Lord your God, that it may be there for a witness against thee.

And thou shalt put the mercy-seat above, upon the ark ; and in the ark thou shalt put the testimony that I shall give thee.

There was a tradition among the Jews that the Book of the Law was lost during the captivity, and that it was among the treasures discovered during the building of the second temple. The same opinion was entertained by the early Christian fathers, such for instance as Irenæus, Tertullian and Clemens Alexandrinus, " for," says Prideaux, " they (the Christian fathers) hold that all the Scriptures were lost and destroyed in the Babylonish captivity, and that Ezra restored them all again by divine revelation."[*] The truth of the tradition is very generally denied by biblical scholars, who attribute its origin to the fact that Ezra collected together the copies of the laws, expurgated them of the errors which had crept into them during the captivity, and arranged a new and correct edition. But the truth or falsity of the legend does not affect the masonic symbolism. The Book of the Law is the will of God, which, lost to us in our darkness, must be recovered as precedent to our learning what is TRUTH. As captives to error, truth is lost to us; when freedom is restored, the first reward will be its discovery.

And Moses said, this is the thing which the Lord commandeth, Fill an omer of the manna, to be kept for your generations ; that they may see the bread wherewith I have fed you in the wilderness, when I brought you forth from the land of

[*] Prideaux's Connection vol. i. p. 329.

Egypt. And Moses said unto Aaron, Take a pot, and put an omer full of manna therein, and lay it up before the Lord, to be kept for your generations. As the Lord commanded Moses, so **Aaron laid it up** before the testimony to be kept.

NUMBERS XVII. 10.

And the Lord said unto Moses, Bring Aaron's rod again before the testimony, to be kept for a token.

In one of the highest degrees of the Ancient and Accepted Rite we find the following explanation of the symbolism of the *key* which is equally applicable to Royal Arch Masonry. "The key demonstrates that having obtained the key to our sublime mysteries, the mason, if he behaves with justice, fervency and zeal to his companions, will soon arrive at the true meaning of the masonic society."

But the symbolism is here still further extended. It is within the sacred pages of the law that this invaluable key is found, which teaches us that it is only in the revelations of the Supreme Architect of the Universe that DIVINE TRUTH is to be discovered.

The following passage of Scripture is read as explanatory of an important mystery:

EXODUS VI. 2, 3.

And GOD spake unto Moses, and said unto him, I am the LORD: and I appeared unto Abraham, unto Isaac, and unto Jacob, by the name of GOD Almighty; but by my name JEHOVAH was I not known to them.

An interesting announciation is now made with grateful thanks to God for the discovery, when the following Ode should be sung, the companions all standing :

ROYAL ARCH ODE

PRIMO.
SECONDO.
BASS.

Joy, the sa - cred law is found,

Now the tem - ple stands com - plete,

Glad - ly let us gath - er round

Where the pon - tiff holds his seat ;

Now he spreads the vol - ume wide.

Open - ing forth its leaves to day,

And the mon - arch by his side

Ga - zes on the bright dis - play.

Joy! the secret *vault* is found,
Full the *sunbeam* falls within,
Pointing darkly under ground,
To the treasure we would win.
They have brought it forth to light,
And again it cheers the earth;
All its leaves are purely bright,
Shining in their newest worth.

This shall be the sacred *mark*
Which shall guide us to the skies,
Bearing, like a *holy ark*,
All the hearts who love to rise;
This shall be the *corner stone*
Which the builders threw away,
But was found the only one
Fitted for the *arch's* stay.

This shall be the *gavel* true,
At whose sound the crowd shall bend,
Giving to the *law* its due;
This shall be the faithful friend;
This the token which shall bring
Kindness to the sick and poor,
Hastening on, on Angel's wing,
To the lone and *darksome door*.

This shall crown the mighty *arch*,
When the temple springs on high,
And the brethren bend their march,
Wafting *incense* to the sky.
Then the solemn strain shall swell
From the bosom and the tongue,
And the Master's glory tell
In the harmony of song.

> Here the exile, o'er the waste,
> Trudging homeward, shall repose;
> All his toils and dangers past,
> Here his long sojournings close.
> Entering through the sacred *veils*,
> To the holy cell he bends;
> Then as sinking Nature fails,
> *Hope* in glad fruition ends.

The High Priest will then invest the candidates with an important secret of the degree, which should always be accompanied with an explanatory lecture.

THE TETRAGRAMMATON.

יהוה

THE name of God, which we, at a venture, pronounce JEHOVAH—and which is called the "Tetragrammaton," (from the Greek *tetra*, four, and *gramma*, letter,) because it consists in Hebrew of four letters, and the "Ineffable name," because it was unlawful to pronounce it, was ever held by the Jews in the most profound veneration. They claim to have derived its origin from the immediate inspiration of the Almighty, who communicated it to Moses, as his especial appellation, to be used only by his chosen people. This communication was first made at the Burning Bush, when God said to the Jewish lawgiver: "Thus shalt thou say unto the children of Israel: Jehovah the God of your fathers, the God of Abraham, the God of Isaac, and the God of Jacob hath sent me unto you: this [Jehovah] is my name forever, and this is my memorial unto all generations." And at a subsequent period, he still more emphatically declared this to be his peculiar name, when he said: "I am *Jehovah:* and I appeared unto Abraham, unto Isaac, and unto Jacob, by the name of *El Shaddai;* but by my name JEHOVAH was I not known unto them."

Ushered to their notice by the utmost solemnity and religious consecration, this name of God became invested among the Israelites with the profoundest veneration and awe. To add to this mysticism, the Kabbalists, by the change of a single letter in the original, read the passage which is, "this is my name forever," as if it had been written, "this is my name to be concealed."

This interpretation, though founded on an error, and probably an intentional one, soon became a precept, and has been strictly obeyed to this day. The word *Jehovah* is never pronounced by a pious Jew, who, whenever he meets with it in Scripture, substitutes for it the word *Adonai* or *Lord*, a practice that has been followed by the translators of the common English version of the Bible with almost Jewish scrupulosity, the word Jehovah in the original being always translated by the word "Lord." The use of this word being thus abandoned, its pronunciation was ultimately lost, since by the peculiar construction of the Hebrew language, which is entirely without vowel letters, the vocal sounds being supplied to the ear by oral teaching, the consonants, which alone constitute the alphabet, can, in their combination, give no possible indication, to one who has not heard it before, of the true pronunciation of any given word.

There was one person, however, who, it is said, was in possession of the proper sound of the letters and the true pronunciation of the word. This was the High Priest, who, receiving it through his predecessor, preserved the recollection of the sound by pronouncing it three times, once a year, on the day of Atonement, when he entered the holy of holies of the tabernacle or the temple.

If the traditions of masonry on this subject are correct, the kings, after the establishment of the monarchy, must sometimes have participated in this privilege, for Solomon is said to have been in possession of the word and to have communicated it to his two colleagues at the building of the temple. The Kabbalists and Talmudists have enveloped this ineffable name of God in a host of mystical superstitions, most of which are as absurd as they are incredible, but all of them tend to show the great veneration that has always been paid to it. Thus they say that it is possessed of **unlimited powers,** and that he who pronounces it shakes heaven and earth, and inspires the very angels with terror and astonishment. The **Rabbins call it** "shem hamphorash," that is to say, "the name that was declared," and they assert that David found it engraved on a stone while digging into the earth.

Besides the tetragrammaton or ineffable word, there are many varieties of the name which have been adopted with almost equal veneration among other nations of antiquity, of which the three following may be offered as instances.

1. JAH. This was the name of God in the Syrian language, and is still retained in some of the Syriac forms of doxology. It is to be found in the 68th Psalm, verse 4: "Extol him that rideth upon the heavens by his name JAH," and also in the Song of Moses, (Exodus xv. 2,) where in the original it is "Jah is my strength and my song."

2. BEL. This was the name of God among many of the eastern nations, and particularly among the Chaldeans. It is also frequently met with in Scripture when allusion is made to the idolatrous worship of the Pagan nations.

3. ON. This was one of the names by which God was worshipped by the Egyptians. It is also alluded to in the sacred writings, as when we are told that Pharaoh gave Joseph for his wife, "Asenath, the daughter of Poti-pherah, priest of On." (Genesis, xli. 45.)

Now all these names of God, which, with many others to be found in the ineffable degrees of masonry, make up a whole system, are eminently symbolical. In fact, the name of God must be taken, in Freemasonry, as the symbol of TRUTH, and then the search for it will be nothing but the search after truth, which is the true end and aim of the masonic science of symbolism. The subordinate names are subordinate modifications of truth, but the ineffable tetragrammaton is the symbol of the sublimity and perfection of divine truth, to which all good masons and all good men are seeking to advance, whether it be by the aid of the theological ladder, or by passing between the pillars of Strength and Establishment, or by wandering in darkness, beset on all sides by dangers, or by traveling, weary and worn, over rough and rugged roads—whatever be the direction of our journey, or how accomplished, *light* and *truth*, the Urim and Thummim, are the ultimate objects of our search and our labor as Freemasons.*

THE TRIANGULAR PLATE OF GOLD.

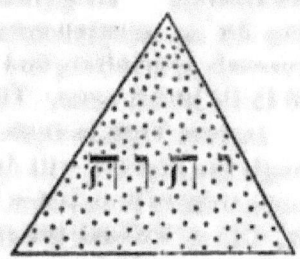

The equilateral triangle was adopted by nearly all the nations of antiquity as a symbol of the Deity. The Egyptians, for instance, considered it as the representative of the great principle of animated existence. Among the Hebrews it was often used as a symbol of the tetragrammaton, and in masonry it retains the same signification, being the symbol of the Grand Architect of the Universe and Bestower of Light, its three sides representing the Past, the Present, and the Future, all of which are contained in the eternal existence of Jehovah.

* See Mackey's Lexicon of Freemasonry, where the words "Jehovah" and "Name of God," will be found to contain information interesting to the Royal Arch Mason.

7

THE CUBICAL STONE.

The cubical stone to which the neophyte is for the first time introduced in this degree is the *Masonic stone of foundation*, which occupies so large and important a portion of the legends and traditions of the order. This stone inscribed with a mystical diagram representing the Ineffable Name, is said to have been in the possession of Adam in Paradise—to have been used by Abel as the altar on which he offered his acceptable sacrifice, and then to have been used for the same purpose by the pious Seth. Enoch subsequently employed it for an important object, and it was finally deposited in the temple of Solomon, for reasons known only to those who have penetrated into the arcana of Freemasonry. Much of this legendary information is altogether of a symbolical character, requiring for its comprehension a thorough acquaintance with masonic symbolism, and is therefore by no means to be taken in its literal sense. These legends are to be met with in the ancient York lectures. The student, in his progress through the degrees, will find repeated references to this "masonic stone of foundation," which supported the ineffable name, with or without the ark, and which may be considered, in whatsoever light we may choose to view the traditions, whether as fabulous or authentic, as really symbolizing Divine Truth, which must alone direct and sustain us in our search after God, whom Freemasons term the Great Architect of the Universe.

The High Priest, after the delivery of the lecture, may conclude the ceremony of exaltation by reading or delivering the following admonitory

CHARGE.

Companions—By the consent and assistance of the members of this Chapter, you are now exalted to the august degree of a Royal Arch Mason. The rites and mysteries developed in this degree, have been handed down through a chosen few, unchanged by time, and uncontrolled by prejudice; and we trust that they will be regarded by you with the same veneration, and transmitted with the same scrupulous purity to your successors.

No one can reflect on the ceremonies of gaining admission into this place, without being forcibly struck with the important lessons which they teach. Here we are necessarily led to contemplate, with gratitude and admiration, the sacred Source from whence all earthly comforts flow. Here we find additional inducements to continue steadfast and immovable in the discharge of our respective duties; and here we are bound by the most solemn ties, to promote each other's welfare, and correct each other's failings, by advice, admonition, and reproof. It is a duty which we owe to our companions of this order, that the application of every candidate for admission should be examined with the most scrutinizing eye, so that we may always possess the satisfaction of finding none among us, but such as will promote, to the utmost of their power, the great end of our institution. By paying due attention to this determination, you will never recommend any candidate for our mysteries, whose abilities and knowledge you cannot freely vouch for and whom you do not firmly and confidently believe, will fully conform to the principles of our order, and fulfil the obligations of a Royal Arch Mason. While such are our members, we may expect to be united in one object, without indifference, inattention or neglect; fervency and zeal, fidelity and affection, will be the distinguishing characteristics of our society; and that satisfaction, harmony and peace, will be enjoyed at our meetings, which no other society can afford.

CLOSING OF THE CHAPTER.

A Chapter of Royal Arch Masons is closed as it was opened, with the most solemn and impressive ceremonies, and that symbol of truth which had been brought forth to be contemplated during the hours of labor being now again deposited, to remain in silence until the craftsmen shall again assemble, the brethren are dismissed with the following.

PRAYER.

By the *wisdom* of the Supreme High Priest, may we be directed; by his *strength*, may we be enabled; and by the *beauty* of virtue, may we be incited, to perform the obligations here enjoined on us; to keep inviolably the mysteries here unfolded to us; and invariably to practice all those duties out of the Chapter, which are inculcated in it. So mote it be. Amen.

ROYAL ARCH HISTORY:

IN THREE LECTURES.

BY ALBERT G. MACKEY, M. D.

———◆———

LECTURE I.

The Destruction of the Temple.

———

"They have cast fire into thy sanctuary; they have defiled by casting down the dwelling place of thy name to the ground.—PSALM lxxiv. 7

———

THERE is no part of sacred history, except perhaps the account of the construction of the temple, which should be more interesting to the advanced mason than that which relates to the destruction of Jerusalem, the captivity of the Jews at Babylon, and the subsequent restoration under Cyrus for the purpose of rebuilding "the house of the Lord." Intimately connected, as the events which are commemorated in this period are, with the organization of the Royal Arch degree, it is impossible that any mason who has been exalted to that degree, can thoroughly understand the nature and bearing of the secrets with which he has been entrusted, unless he shall have devoted some portion of time to the study of the historical incidents to which these secrets refer.

The history of the Jewish people from the death of Solomon to the final destruction of the temple, was one continued series of civil dissensions among themselves, and of revolts in government and apostacies in religion. No sooner had Rehoboam, the son and successor of Solomon, ascended the throne, than his harsh and tyrannical conduct so incensed the people that ten of the tribes revolted from his authority, and placing themselves under the government of Jeroboam, the son of Nebat, formed the separate kingdom of Israel, while Rehoboam continued to rule over the tribes of Judah and Benjamin, which thenceforth constituted the kingdom of Israel, whose capital remained at Jerusalem. From thenceforward the history of Palestine becomes two-fold. The ten revolting tribes which constituted the Is-raelitish monarchy, soon formed a schismatic religion, which eventually terminated in idolatry, and caused their final ruin and dispersion. But the two remaining tribes proved hardly more faithful to the God of their fathers, and carried their idolatry to such an extent, that at length there was scarcely a town in all Judea that did not have its tutelary deity borrowed from the idolatrous gods of its pagan neighbors. Even in Jerusalem, "the holy city," the prophet Jeremiah tells us that altars were set up to Baal. Israel was the first to receive its punishment for this career of wickedness, and the ten tribes were carried into a cap-tivity from which they never returned. As a nation, they have been stricken from the roll of history.

But this wholesome example was lost upon Judea. The destruction of the ten tribes by no means impeded the pro-gress of the other two towards idolatry and licentiousness. Judah and Benjamin, however, were never without a line of prophets, priests, and holy men, whose teachings and exhortations sometimes brought the apostate Jews back to their first allegiance, and for a brief period restored the pure theism of the Mosaic dispensation.

Among these bright but evanescent intervals of regen-eracy, we are to account the pious reign of the good King Josiah, during which the altars of idolatry throughout his kingdom were destroyed, the temple was repaired, and its regular service restored. It was in the prosecution of this laudable duty, that a copy of the Book of the Law, which had long been lost, was found in a crypt of the temple, and after having been publicly read to the priests, the levites, and the people, it was again, by the direction of the pro-phetess Huldah, deposited in a secret place.

But notwithstanding this fortuitous discovery of the Book of the Law, and notwithstanding all the efforts of King Josiah to reëstablish the worship of his fathers, the Jews were so attached to the practices of idolatry, that upon his death, being encouraged by his son and successor Jehoahaz, who was an impious monarch, they speedily returned to the adoration of pagan deities and the observance of pagan rites.

The forbearance of God was at length exhausted, and in the reign of this King Jehoahaz, the series of divine punishments commenced, which only terminated in the destruction of Jerusalem and the captivity of its inhabitants.

The instrument selected by the Deity for carrying out his designs in the chastisement of the idolatrous Jews, was Nebuchadnezzar, King of the Chaldees, then reigning at Babylon; and as this monarch, and the country which he governed, played an important part in the series of events which are connected with the organization of the Royal Arch degree, it is necessary that we should here pause in the narrative in which we have been engaged, to take a brief view of the locality of Babylon, the seat of the captivity, and of the history of the Chaldee nation, whose leader was the conqueror of Judah.

"Few countries of antiquity," says Heeren,[*] "have so just a claim to the attention of the historian as Babylonia." The fertility of its soil, the wealth of its inhabitants, the splendor of its cities, the refinement of its society, continued to give it a pre-eminent renown through a succession of ages. It occupied a narrow strip of land, lying between the river Tigris on the east and the Euphrates on the west, and extending about five hundred and forty miles west of north. The early inhabitants were undoubtedly of the Shemitic race, deriving their existence from one common origin with the Hebrews, though it is still a question with the historian whether they originally came from India or

---

[*] Historical Researches into the Politics, Intercourse, and Trade of the principal nations of antiquity, vol. i. p. 371.

from the peninsula of Arabia.* They originally formed a part of the great Assyrian monarchy, but their early history having no connection with Royal Arch Masonry, may be passed over without further discussion. About six hundred and thirty years before the Christian era, Babylon, the chief city, was conquered by Nebuchadnezzar, the King of the Chaldeans, a nomadic race, who descending from their homes in the mountains of Taurus and Caucasus, between the Euxine and the Caspian seas, overwhelmed the countries of Southern Asia, and became masters of the Syrian and Babylonian empires.

Nebuchadnezzar was a warlike monarch, and during his reign was engaged in many contests for the increase of his power and the extension of his dominions. Among other nations who fell beneath his victorious arms, was Judea, whose King Jehoahaz, or as he was afterwards named Jehoiakim, was compelled to purchase peace by paying an annual tribute to his conquerors. Jehoiakim was subsequently slain by Nebuchadnezzar, and his son Jehoiachin ascended the throne of Israel. The oppression of the Babylonians still continued, and after a reign of three months, Jehoiachin was deposed by the King of the Chaldees, and his kingdom given to his uncle Zedekiah, a monarch who is characterized by Josephus as "a despiser of justice and his duty."

It was in the reign of this ungodly sovereign that the incidents took place which are commemorated in the first part of the Royal Arch degree. Having repeatedly rebelled against the authority of the Babylonian king, to whose appointment he was indebted for his throne, Nebuchadnezzar repaired with an army to Judea, and laying siege to Jerusalem, after a severe struggle of eighteen months' duration, reduced it. He then caused the city to be leveled with the ground, the royal palace to be burned, the temple

---

* Historical Researches into the Politics, Intercourse and Trade of the principal nations of antiquity, vol. i. p. 381.

to be pillaged, and the inhabitants to be carried captive to Babylon.

These events are symbolically detailed in the Royal Arch, and in allusion to them, the passage of the Book of Chronicles which records them, is appropriately read during the ceremonies of this part of the degree.

"Zedekiah was one-and-twenty years old when he began to reign, and reigned eleven years in Jerusalem. And he did that which was evil in the sight of the Lord his God, and humbled not himself before Jeremiah the prophet speaking from the mouth of the Lord. And he also rebelled against King Nebuchadnezzar, and stiffened his neck, and hardened his heart from turning unto the Lord God of Israel. Moreover, all the chief of the priests and the people transgressed very much after all the abominations of the heathen; and polluted the house of the Lord, which he had hallowed in Jerusalem, and the Lord God of their fathers sent to them by his messengers, because he had compassion on his people and on his dwelling place. But they mocked the messengers of God, and despised his words, and misused his prophets, until the wrath of the Lord arose against his people, till there was no remedy."

This preparatory clause announces the moral causes which led to the destruction of Jerusalem—the evil counsels and courses of Zedekiah,—his hardness of heart,—his willful deafness to the denunciations of the Lord's prophet, —and his violation of all his promises of obedience to Nebuchadnezzar. But not to the king alone was confined this sinfulness of life. The whole of the people, and even the priests, the very servants of the the house of the Lord, were infected with the moral plague. They had abandoned the precepts and observances of their fathers, which were to have made them a peculiar people, and falling into the idolatries of their heathen neighbors, had desecrated the altars of Jehovah with the impure fire of strange gods. Message after message had been sent to them from that

7*

God who had properly designated himself as "long suffering and abundant in goodness"—but all was in vain. The threats and warnings of the prophets were heard with contempt, and the messengers of God were treated with contumely, and hence the fatal result which is detailed in the succeeding passages of Scripture read before the candidate.

"Therefore he brought upon them the King of the Chaldees, who slew their young men with the sword, in the house of their sanctuary, and had no compassion upon young man or maiden, old man or him that stooped for age; he gave them all into his hand. And all the vessels of the house of God, great and small, and the treasures of the house of the Lord, and the treasures of the king and of his princes; all these he brought to Babylon."

But the king of the Chaldees was not content with the rich spoils of war that he had gained. It was not sufficient that the sacred vessels of the temple, made by order of King Solomon, and under the supervision of that "curious and cunning workman," who had "adorned and beautified the edifice" erected for the worship of Jehovah, should become the prey of an idolatrous monarch. The dark sins of the people and the king required a heavier penalty. The very house of the Lord itself—that sacred building which had been erected on the "threshing floor of Ornan the Jebusite," and which constituted the third Grand Offering of Masonry on the same sacred place, was to be burned to its foundations; the city which was consecrated by its presence was to be leveled to the ground; and its inhabitants were to be led into a long and painful captivity. Hence the tale of devastation proceeds as follows:

"And they burnt the house of God, and brake down the wall of Jerusalem, and burnt all the palaces thereof with fire; and destroyed all the goodly vessels thereof. And them that had escaped from the sword carried he away captive to Babylon; where they were servants to him and his sons until the reign of the kingdom of Persia."

These events took place in the year 588 before Christ. But we must not suppose this to have been the beginning of the "seventy years' captivity" foretold by the prophet Jeremiah. That actually commenced eighteen years before, in the reign of Jehoiakim, when Daniel was among the captives. Counting from the destruction of Jerusalem under Zedekiah, which is the event recorded in the Royal Arch, to the termination of the captivity under Cyrus, we shall have but fifty-two years, so that we may readily understand how there should be among the aged men assembled to see the foundations laid of the second temple, many who had beheld the splendor and magnificence of the first.

But though the city was destroyed, and the temple burnt, the deep foundations of the latter were not destroyed. The ark of the covenant, with the book of the law which it contained, was undoubtedly destroyed in the general conflagration, for we read no account of its having been carried to Babylon, but the wisdom and foresight of Solomon had made a provision four hundred and seventy years before, for the safe preservation of an exact image of that sacred chest.

Thus we terminate what may be called the first section of the Royal Arch degree. The sound of war has been upon the nation—the temple is overthrown—the city is become a desert—yet even in its desolation, magnificent in its ruins of palaces and stupendous edifices—and the people have been dragged in chains as captives to Babylon.

LECTURE II.

The Captivity at Babylon.

"By the rivers of Babylon, there we sat down; yea, we wept when we remembered Zion. We hanged our harps upon the willows in the midst thereof."—PSALM CXXXVII. 1–2.

BETWEEN that portion of the ritual of the Royal Arch which refers to the destruction of the first temple, and that subsequent part which symbolizes the building of the second, there is an interregnum (if we may be allowed the term) in the ceremonial of the degree, which must be considered as a long interval in history, the filling up of which, like the interval between the acts of a play, must be left to the imagination of the spectator. This interval represents the time passed in the captivity of the Jews at Babylon. That captivity lasted for seventy years, from the reign of Nebuchadnezzar until that of Cyrus, although but fifty-two of these years are commemorated in the Royal Arch degree. During this period many circumstances of great interest and importance occurred, which must be perfectly understood to enable us to appreciate the concluding portion of the ceremonies of that degree.

"Babylon the great," as the prophet Daniel calls it, the city to which the captive Jews were conducted by Nebuchadnezzar, was situated four hundred and seventy-five miles in a nearly due east direction from Jerusalem. It stood in the midst of a large and fertile plain on each side of the river Euphrates, which ran through it from north to south. It was surrounded with walls which were eighty-seven feet thick, three hundred and fifty in height, and sixty miles in compass. These were all built of large bricks, cemented together with bitumen. Exterior to the walls was a wide and deep trench, lined with the same material. Twenty-five gates on each side, made of solid brass, gave admission to the city. From each of these gates proceeded a wide street, fifteen miles in length, and the whole was separated by means of other smaller divisions, and contained six hundred and seventy-six squares, each of which was two miles and a quarter in circumference. Two hundred and fifty towers, placed upon the walls, afforded the means of additional strength and protection. Within this immense circuit were to be found palaces and temples and other edifices of the utmost magnificence, which have caused the wealth, the luxury and the splendor of Babylon to become the favorite theme of the historians of antiquity, and which compelled the prophet Isaiah, even while denouncing its downfall, to speak of it as "the glory of kingdoms, the beauty of the Chaldees' excellency."

To this city the captives were conducted. What was the exact number removed we have no means of ascertaining. We are led to believe from certain passages of Scripture that the deportation was not complete.* Calmet says that Nebuchadnezzar carried away only the principal inhabitants, the warriors and artizans of every kind (which would, of course, include the masons), and that he left the husbandmen, the laborers, and, in general, the poorer classes that constituted the great body of the people. Among the prisoners of distinction, Josephus mentions the high priest, Seraiah, and Zephaniah, the priest that was next him, with the three rulers that guarded the temple, the eunuch who was over the armed men, seven friends of Zedekiah, his scribe and sixty other rulers. Zedekiah, the king, had attempted to escape, previous to the termination of the siege, but being pursued was captured and carried to Riblah, the headquarters of Nebuchadnezzar, where, having first been compelled to behold the slaughter of his children, his eyes were then put out, and he was conducted in chains to Babylon.†

---

* Jeremiah (li. 16) says that Nebuzaradan left "certain of the poor of the land for vine-dressers and for husbandmen."

† These circumstances are detailed in the degree of "Super Excellent Mas-

A masonic tradition informs us that the captive Jews were bound by their conquerors with triangular chains, and that this was done by the Chaldeans as an additional insult, because the Jewish masons were known to esteem the triangle as an emblem of the sacred name of God, and must have considered its appropriation to the form of their fetters as a desecration of the Tetragrammaton.

Of the road pursued by the Chaldeans with their prisoners we can judge only from conjecture. It is, however, recorded that they were carried by Nebuzaradan, the captain of Nebuchadnezzar's army, direct from Jerusalem to Riblah, where Nebuchadnezzar had fixed his headquarters. Riblah **was situated** on the northern border of Palestine, about two hundred miles northeast of Jerusalem, and was the city through which the Babylonians were accustomed to pass in their eruptions into and departures from Judea.

From Jerusalem to Riblah, the journey is necessarily through Damascus, and the route from Riblah was direct to Palmyra. Hence, we have every reason for supposing that the Chaldean army, with the captives, took that route which is described by Heeren*, and which would have conducted them from Jerusalem, through Damascus, to Riblah in a northerly direction. Here Nebuchadnezzar commanded Seraiah the high priest, and the rulers, to the amount of seventy, to be put to death. Thence directing their course to the north-east, they arrived at Thapsacus, an important commercial town on the Euphrates, which river they crossed somewhat lower down at a place called Circesium. They then journeyed in a southerly direction, through the Median wall and along the east bank of the Euphrates to Babylon. By this route they avoided making

---

ter"—a degree not used in **our chapters.** The tradition of this degree says that the thumbs of Zedekiah **were cut off, but this additional** punishment is not mentioned either by Jeremiah or Josephus.

* In his Appendix "on the Commercial Routes of Ancient Asia," affixed to his Historical Researches.—*Append.* xiii. ii. 2.

a large circuit to the north, or crossing an extensive desert which could supply no water.

The condition of Jerusalem after the departure of the captives is worthy of consideration. Previous to his departure from Jerusalem, Nebuzaradan appointed Gedaliah, who was the son of Ahikam, a person of an illustrious family, governor of the remnant of the Jews who were left behind. Gedaliah is described by the Jewish historian as being of "a gentle and righteous disposition." He established his seat of government at Mispah, and induced those who had fled during the siege, and who were scattered over the country, to return and cultivate the land, promising them protection and favor if they consented to continue peaceable and pay a small tribute to the king of Babylon.

Among those who had fled on the approach of the Chaldean army was Ishmael, one of the royal family, a wicked and crafty man, who, during the siege of Jerusalem, had sought protection at the court of the King of the Ammorites. Ishmael was secretly instigated by Bealis; the Ammoritish monarch, to slay Gedaliah, that, as one of the royal family, he might himself ascend the throne of David. Notwithstanding that Gedaliah was informed of this nefarious design, he refused, in his unsuspecting temper, to believe the report, and consequently fell a victim to the treachery of Ishmael, who slew him while partaking of his hospitality. Ishmael then attempted to carry the inhabitants of Mispah into captivity, and fled with them to the king of the Ammorites; but being overtaken by the friends of Gedaliah, who had armed themselves to avenge his death, the captives were rescued and Ishmael put to flight. The Jews, fearing that if they remained they would be punished by the Babylonians for the murder of Gedaliah, retired to Egypt. Five years after, Nebuchadnezzar, having invaded and conquered Egypt, carried all the Jews whom he found there to Babylon. "And such," says Josephus, "was the end of the nation of the Hebrews." Jerusalem was now desolate. Its king and its people were removed to Babylon, but it remained unpopulated by foreign colonies, perhaps, as Whiston suggests, "as an indication of Providence that the Jews were to re-people it without opposition themselves."

Let us turn now to the more immediate object of this lecture, and examine the condition of the captives during their sojourn in Babylon.

Notwithstanding the ignominious mode of their conveyance from Jerusalem, and the vindictiveness displayed by their conqueror in the destruction of their city and temple, they do not appear, on their arrival at Babylon, to have been subjected to any of the extreme rigors of slavery. They were distributed into various parts of the empire; some remaining in the city, while others were sent into the provinces. The latter probably devoted themselves to agricultural pursuits, while the former were engaged in commerce or in the labors of architecture. Anderson says, that Nebuchadnezzar, having applied himself to the design of finishing his buildings at Babylon, engaged therein all the able artists of Judea and other captives to join his own Chaldean masons.* They were permitted to retain their personal property, and even to purchase lands and erect houses. Their civil and religious government was not utterly destroyed, for they retained a regular succession of kings and high priests, one of each of whom returned with them, as will be seen hereafter, on their restoration. Some of the principal captives were advanced to offices of dignity and power in the royal palace, and were permitted to share in the councils of state. Their prophets, Daniel and Ezekiel, with their associates, preserved among their countrymen the pure doctrines of their religion, and taught that belief in the Divine Being which constituted the most important principle of Primitive Freemasonry, in opposition to the spurious system practised by their idolatrous conquerors. "The people," says Oliver, "who adhered to the worship of God, and they were neither

---

* Book of Constitutions, p, 17, edit. 1723.

few nor insignificant, continued to meet in their schools, or lodges, for the undisturbed practice of their system of ethical Freemasonry, which they did not fail to propagate for their mutual consolation during this calamitous reverse of fortune, and for the benefit of their descendants."*

The rabbinical writers inform us that during the captivity a fraternity was established, for the preservation of traditional knowledge, which was transmitted to a few initiates, and that on the restoration, Zerubbabel, Joshua and Esdras carried all this secret instruction to Jerusalem, and there established a similar fraternity. The principal seats of this institution were at Naharda, on the Euphrates, at Sora, and at Pompeditha."†

Among the remarkable events that occurred during the captivity, we are to account the visit of Pythagoras to Babylon. This ancient philosopher was, while in Egypt, taken prisoner by Cambyses, during his invasion of that country, and carried to Babylon, where he remained for twelve years. There he is said to have had frequent interviews with Ezekiel, and to have derived from the instructions of the prophet much of that esoteric system of philosophy into which he afterwards indoctrinated his disciples.

Jehoiachin, who had been the king of Judah before Zedekiah, and had been dethroned and carried as a captive to Babylon, remained in prison for thirty-seven years, during the long reign of Nebuchadnezzar. But at the death of that monarch, his son and successor, Evilmerodach, restored the captive king to liberty, and promoted him to great honor in his palace. Evilmerodach, who was infamous for his vices, reigned only two years, when he was deposed and put to death by his own relations, and Neriglissar, his sis-

---

* Historical Landmarks, vol ii. p. 410.

† See Mackey's Lexicon of Freemasonry, word *Naharda*. It is but fair to remark that the authors of the "Encyclopedie Methodique," in common with many other writers, place the establishment of these colleges at a much later date, and subsequent to the Christian era. But Oliver supposes them to have been founded during the captivity.

ter's husband, ascended the throne. Jehoiachin is said to have died at the same time, or, as Prideaux conjectures, he was, as the favorite of Evilmerodach, slain with him.

After the death of Jehoiachin, Salathiel or Shealtiel, his son, became the "head of the captivity," or **nominally the** Jewish king.

Neriglissar, or Niglissar, as he is called by Josephus, reigned for forty years, and then was succeeded by his son Labosordacus. This monarch became by his crimes hateful to the people, and, after a short reign of only nine months, was slain by his own subjects. The royal line, whose throne had been usurped by Neriglissar, was then restored in the **person** of Belshazzar, **one** of the descendants of Nebuchadnezzar. Belshazzar was an effeminate and licentious monarch, indulging in luxury and dissipation, while the reins of government were entrusted to his mother, Nitocris. He was, therefore, but ill prepared by temper or ability to oppose the victorious arms of Cyrus, the King of Persia, and Darius, the King of Media, who made war upon him. Consequently, after an inglorious reign of seventeen years, his power was wrested from him, the city of Babylon was taken by Cyrus, and the Babylonian power was forever annihilated.

After the death of Shealtiel, the sovereignty of the Jews was transmitted to his son, Zerubbabel, who thus became the head of the captivity, or normal Prince of Judea.

While the line of the Jewish monarchs was thus preserved, during the captivity, in the house of David, the Jews were **not** less careful to maintain the due succession of the high priesthood; for Jehosadek, the son of Seraiah, was the high priest that was carried by Nebuchadnezzar to Babylon, and when he died, during the captivity, he was succeeded in his sacred office by his eldest son, Joshua.

In the first year of the reign of Cyrus the captivity of the Jews was terminated. Cyrus, from his conversations with Daniel and the other Jewish captives of learning and piety, as well as from his perusal of their sacred books,

more especially the prophecies of Isaiah, had become im-
bued with a knowledge of true religon, and hence had even
publicly announced to his subjects his belief in the God
"which the nation of the Israelites worshiped." He was
consequently impressed with an earnest desire to fulfill the
prophetic declarations, of which he was the subject, and to
re-build the temple of Jerusalem. Accordingly, he issued
a proclamation, which we find in Ezra, as follows:

"Thus saith Cyrus, King of Persia, The Lord God of
heaven hath given me all the kingdoms of the earth; and
he hath charged me to build him a house at Jerusalem,
which is in Judea. Who is there among you of all his people? his God be with him, and let him go up to Jerusalem,
which is in Judea, and build the house of the Lord God of
Israel, (he is the God,) which is in Jerusalem."

With the publication of this proclamation of Cyrus, commences what may be called the second part of the Royal
Arch degree. The whole space of time occupied in the
captivity, and the events connected with that portion of the
Jewish history, are not referred to in the ceremonies, but
constitute, as we have already remarked, an interval like
the period of time supposed to pass in a drama, between
the falling of a curtain at the close of one act and its being
raised at the commencement of the subsequent one. But
now there are "glad tidings of great joy," as given in this
proclamation to the Jews. The captives are liberated—the
exiles are permitted to return home. Leaving the banks
of the Euphrates, they direct their anxious steps over *rough
and rugged roads* to that beloved mountain of the Lord,
where their ancestors were so long wont to worship. The
events connected with this restoration are of deep attrac-
tion to the mason, since the history abounds in interesting
and instructive legends. But the importance of the subject demands that we should pursue the investigation in a
separate lecture.

LECTURE III.

The Return to Jerusalem.

"For, lo, the days come, saith the Lord, that I will bring again the captivity of my people Israel and Judah, saith the Lord ; and I will cause them to return to the land that I gave to their fathers, and they shall possess it.'
JEREMIAH XXX. 3.

WE have now arrived at that portion of the history of the Babylonish captivity which is allegorized in the concluding ceremonies of the Royal Arch degree. And here we may incidentally observe, that the same analogy which exists in the Master's degree to the ancient mysteries, is also to be found in the Royal Arch. The masonic scholar, who is familiar with the construction of those mysteries of the Pagan priests and philosophers, is well aware that they inculcate by symbolic and allegoric instruction, the great lessons of the resurrection of the body and the immortality of the soul. Hence they were all funereal in their character. They commenced in sorrow, they terminated in joy. The death or destruction of some eminent personage, most generally a god, was depicted in the beginning of the ceremonies of initiation, while the close was occupied in illustrating, in the same manner, the discovery of his grave, the recovery of the body, and the restoration to life eternal. The same religious instruction is taught in the Master's degree. The evidence of this fact, it is unnecessary for us here to demonstrate. It will be at once apparent to every mason who is sufficiently acquainted with the ritual of his order.

But is it not equally apparent that the same system, though under a thicker veil, is preserved in the ceremonies of the Royal Arch ? There is a resurrection of that which has been buried—a discovery of that which had been lost—an exchange of that which, like the body, the earthly tenement, was temporary, for that which, like the soul, is intended to be permanent. The life which we pass on earth is but a *substitute* for that glorious one which we are to spend in eternity. And it is in the grave, in the depths of the earth, that the corruptible puts on incorruption, that the mortal puts on immortality,* and that the substitute of this temporal life is exchanged for the blessed reality of life eternal.

The interval to which we alluded in the last lecture, and which is occupied by the captivity of the Jews at Babylon, is now over, and the allegory of the Royal Arch is resumed with the restoration of the captives to their home.

Five hundred and thirty-six years before the Christian era, Cyrus issued his decree for the return of the Jews. At the same time he restored to them all the sacred vessels and precious ornaments of the first temple, which had been carried away by Nebuchadnezzar, and which were still in existence.

Forty-two thousand three hundred and sixty of the Jews repaired, in the same year, from Babylon and the neighboring cities to Jerusalem. The leaders of these were Zerubbabel, Joshua and Haggai, of whom, as they perform an important part in the history of this event as recorded in the Royal Arch, it is incumbent on us to speak more particularly.†

Zerubbabel was, at the time of the restoration, the possessor of the regal authority among the Jews, as the prince of the captivity and a descendant of the house of David, and as such he assumed at Jerusalem the office of king. He was the son of Shealtiel, who was the son of Jechoniah, the monarch who had been deposed by Nebuchadnezzar and carried away to Babylon. He was the intimate friend of Cyrus, and indeed, it is supposed that it was principally through his influence that the Persian monarch was induced to decree the liberation of the captives.

---

* I. Corinth. xv. 53.

† In the English ritual of the Royal Arch, Ezra and Nehemiah are added to the number as scribes.

Joshua, the High Priest, was, like Zerubbabel, entitled to his office by the indisputable claim of direct descent from the ancient hierarchy. He was the son of Josedech, and the grandson of Seraiah, who had been the High Priest when Jerusalem was taken by Nebuchadnezzar.

Of Haggai, the Scribe, but little is known that can be relied on. We know nothing of the place or the time of his birth, but it is supposed that he was born at Babylon during the captivity. He was the first of the three prophets who flourished after the captivity, and his writings, though few, (so few, indeed, that some theologians have supposed that the larger portion of them has perished,) all relate to the building of the second temple. The office of scribe, which is the one assigned to him in the Royal Arch degree, was one of great importance in the Jewish economy. The *sophers* or scribes constituted, says Dr. Beard,* a learned, organized, much esteemed and highly influential body of men, recognized and supported by the state." They were learned in the laws, and it was their duty to expound them to the people. Horne† says that the scribe seems to have been the king's secretary of state, and as such to have registered all acts and decrees. It is, perhaps, in this capacity that we are to suppose that Haggai claims a place in the Grand Council of the Royal Arch.

Zerubbabel, assisted by these advisers, proceeded to arrange his followers in such a form as would enable them most safely and expeditiously to traverse the long and dangerous road from Babylon to Jerusalem, which latter place they reached after a journey of four months, on the 22d of June, 535 years before the birth of Christ.

The first object of the Jewish leader was, we may well suppose, to provide the means of shelter for the people who accompanied him. We are irresistibly led to the conclusion that for this purpose it was found necessary to erect tents

---

* In Kitto's Cyclop. of Bib. Literat., art. *Scribe.*

† Introduct. to Crit. Stud. and Knowl. of Script., vol. iii. p. 93.

for their temporary dwelling. Extensive and populous as was Jerusalem at the commencement of the captivity, after the ruthless devastation of its unsparing conqueror it could hardly have retained sufficient means for the convenient accommodation of the fifty thousand souls who were thus suddenly and unexpectedly brought within its walls. Tents, therefore, afforded rude and temporary dwellings, until, in the course of time, more substantial buildings could be erected.

The next thing was to restore the ancient sacrifices and religious services, and for this purpose to provide a temporary place of worship until the second temple could be completed. Accordingly, a few months after their arrival, they met together at Jerusalem and celebrated the Feast of Trumpets, and a few days subsequently, the Feast of Tabernacles. It was probably the celebration of this latter observance, as well as the necessity and expediency of the measure, that led the Grand Council of leaders to the erection of a temporary tabernacle near the ruins of the ancient temple, the existence of which is so familiar to us from the traditions and ceremonies of the Royal Arch.

Having thus furnished dwellings for the workmen, and a sacred edifice for the celebration of their religious rites, our Masonic traditions inform us that Joshua, the High Priest, Zerubbabel, the King, and Haggai the Scribe, daily sat in council, to devise plans for the workmen and to superintend the construction of the new temple, which, like a phœnix, was to arise from the ashes of the former one.

It is this period of time in the history of the second temple, that is commemorated in the concluding portion of the Royal Arch. The ruins of the ancient temple are begun to be removed, and the foundations of the second are laid. Joshua, Zerubbabel and Haggai are sitting in daily council within the tabernacle; parties of Jews who had not left Babylon with the main body under Zerubbabel, are continually coming up to Jerusalem to assist in rebuilding the house of the Lord.

During this period of laborious activity a circumstance occurred, which is alluded to in the ritual of the Royal Arch. The Samaritans were desirous of assisting the Jews in the construction of the temple, but their propositions were at once rejected by Zerubbabel. To understand the cause of this refusal to receive their coöperation, we must for a moment advert to the history of this people.

The ten tribes who had revolted from Rehoboam, the son of Solomon, and who had chosen Jeroboam for their king, rapidly fell into idolatry, and having selected the town of Samaria for their metropolis, a complete separation was thus effected between the kingdoms of Judah and Israel. Subsequently, the Samaritans were conquered by the Assyrians under Shalmanezer, who carried the greater part of the inhabitants into captivity, and introduced colonies in their place from Babylon, Cultah, Ava, Hamath and Sepharvaim. These colonists, who assumed the name of Samaritans, brought with them, of course, the idolatrous creed and practices of the region from which they emigrated. The Samaritans, therefore, at the time of the rebuilding of the second temple, were an idolatrous race,* and as such abhorrent to the Jews. Hence, when they asked permission to assist in the pious work of rebuilding the temple, Zerub-

---

* They were not, perhaps, altogether idolators, although idolatry was the predominant religion. The Rev. Dr. Davidson says of them:

"It appears that the people were a mixed race. The greater part of the Israelites had been carried away captive by the Assyrians, including the rich, the strong, and such as were able to bear arms. But the poor and the feeble had been left. The country had not been so entirely depopulated as to possess no Israelite whatever. The dregs of the populace, particularly those who appeared incapable of active service, were not taken away by the victors. With them, therefore, the heathen colonists became incorporated. But the latter were far more numerous than the former, and had all power in their own hands. The remnant of the Israelites was so inconsiderable and insignificant as not to affect, to any important extent, the opinions of the new inhabitants. As the people were a *mixed* race, their religion also assumed a *mixed* character. In it the worship of idols was associated with that of the true God. But apostacy from Jehovah was not universal." See the article **Samaritans** in Kitto's "Cyclopedia of Biblical Literature."

babel, with the rest of the leaders, replied, " Ye have nothing to do with us to build a house unto our God ; but we ourselves together will build unto the Lord God of Israel, as King Cyrus, the King of Persia has commanded us."*

Hence it was that, to avoid the possibility of these idolatrous Samaritans polluting the holy work by their coöperation, Zerubbabel found it necessary to demand of every one who offered himself as an assistant in the undertaking, that he should give an accurate account of his lineage, and prove himself to have been a descendant (which no Samaritan could be) of those faithful Giblemites who worked at the building of the first temple.

It was while the workmen were engaged in making the necessary excavations for laying the foundation, and while numbers continued to arrive at Jerusalem from Babylon, that three worn and weary sojourners, after plodding on foot over the rough and devious roads between the two cities, offered themselves to the Grand Council as willing participants in the labor of erection. Who these sojourners were, we have no historical means of discovering; but there is a Masonic tradition (entitled, perhaps, to but little weight) that they were Hananiah, Misael and Azariah, three holy men, who are better known to general readers by their Chaldaic names of Shadrach, Mesheck and Abednego, as having been miraculously preserved from the fiery furnace of Nebuchadnezzar.

Their services were accepted, and from their diligent labors resulted that important discovery, the perpetuation and preservation of which constitutes the great end and design of the Royal Arch degree.

This ends the connection of the history of the restoration with that of the Royal Arch. The works were soon after suspended in consequence of difficulties thrown in the way by the Samaritans, and other circumstances occurred to pre-

* Ezra, iv. 3.

8

vent the final completion of the temple for many years subsequent to the important discovery to which we have just alluded. But these details go beyond the Royal Arch, and are to be found in the higher degrees of Masonry, such as the Red Cross Knight and the Prince of Jerusalem.

END OF THE ROYAL ARCH DEGREE.

BOOK V.

High Priesthood.

"Melchizedek had preserved in his family and among his subjects the worship of the true God and the primitive patriarchal institutions: by these the father of every family was both king and priest; so Melchizedek being a worshiper of the true God, was priest among the people as well as king over them."

ADAM CLARKE ON GENESIS.

ORDER OF HIGH PRIESTHOOD.

SYMBOLICAL DESIGN.

THE design of this degree, so far as it relates to its symbolic ceremonies, appears to be to present to the candidate the bond of brotherly love which should unite those who, having been elevated to the highest station by their companions, are thus engaged in one common task of preserving the landmarks of the order unimpaired, and in protecting, by their high authority, the integrity and honor of the institution. Thus, separated from the general mass of laborers in the field of masonry, and consecrated to a sacred mission as teachers of its glorious truths, those who sit in the tabernacle as the representatives of the ancient high priesthood, are, by the impressive ceremonies of this degree, reminded of the intimate friendship and fellowship which should exist between all those who have been honored with this distinguished privilege.

HISTORICAL SUMMARY

IT is impossible, from the want of authentic documents, to throw much light upon the historical origin of this degree. No allusion to it can be found in any ritual works out of America, nor even here anterior to about the end of the last and beginning of this century. Webb is the first who mentions it, and gives it a place in the series of capitular degrees. It is probable that it was established by Webb, at the same time that he gave that form to the Prestonian lectures, and ceremonies of the inferior degrees which have since so universally obtained in this country. If so, we may make a guess, and a guess only, at the source whence he derived his general idea of the degree. In 1780, a masonic rite was founded at Berlin, Prussia, called the "Initiated Brothers of Asia."* It was a philosophical rite, intended to give what was supposed to be a true explanation of all masonic symbolism. The fifth degree of this rite was entitled "Melchizedek, or the Royal Priest." It is possible that this degree may have suggested to Webb his idea of the "Order of High Priesthood."

CONSTITUTIONAL PROVISIONS.

THIS order is an honorarium or gift of honor to be bestowed upon the High Priest of a Royal Arch Chapter, and consequently no one is legally entitled to receive it, until he has been duly elected to preside as High Priest in a regular Chapter of Royal Arch Masons. This order should not be conferred when a less number than three duly qualified High Priests are present. Whenever the ceremony is performed in due and ample form, the assistance of at least nine High Priests, who have received it, is requisite.

Though the High Priest of every regular Royal Arch

---

* Two works on the subject of the *Brothers of Asia* were printed at Berlin in 1787. Their titles are at No. 225 and 226 of Thory's Catalogue. A sight of either of them would probably set the question at rest.

Chapter, having himself been duly qualified, can confer the order, under the preceding limitation as to number ; yet it is desirable, when circumstances will permit, that it should be conferred by the Grand High Priest of the Grand Royal Arch Chapter, or such Present or Past High Priest as he may designate for that purpose. A convention, notified to meet at the time of any convocation of the Grand Chapter, will afford the best opportunity of conferring this important and exalted order, with appropriate solemnity. Whenever it is conferred, the following directions are to be observed.

A candidate desirous of receiving the order of High Priesthood, makes a written request to his predecessor in office, or, when it can be done, to the Grand High Priest, respectfully requesting that a convention of High Priests may be called, for the purpose of conferring on him the order. When the convention meets, and is duly organized, a certificate of the due election of the candidate to the office of High Priest, must be produced. This certificate is signed by his predecessor in office, attested by the Secretary of the Chapter. On examination of this certificate, the qualifications of the candidate are ascertained, and he is to be elected only by the unanimous votes of all present. The solemn ceremonies of conferring the order upon him then ensue. When ended the presiding officer directs the Secretary of the convention to make a record of the proceedings, and return it to the Secretary of the Grand Chapter, to be by him laid before the Grand High Priest, for the information of all whom it may concern. The convention of High Priests is then dissolved in due form.

It is the duty of every Companion, as soon after his election to the office of High Priest, as is consistent with his personal convenience, to apply for admission to the order of High Priesthood, that he may be fully qualified properly to govern his Chapter. The General Grand Chapter of the United States says, that although it is highly expedient that every High Priest should receive the order, yet its possession is not essentially necessary as a qualification for the discharge of his official duties.

OPENING OF THE CONVENTION.

THE meeting of a body of High Priests for the **purpose** of conferring this degree is called a " Convention."

In some states, as Missouri, Kentucky, Ohio and California, permanent Councils have been organized ; but in **general the organization is a temporary** one, and is dissolved as soon as the business **of** conferring the order on the candidates who may have applied, has been concluded.

But four officers appear essentially necessary, a President, a Secretary, a Conductor, and a Sentinel or Guard ; but that the ceremonies may be conferred in the most ample form, it is usual in many jurisdictions, especially in those which have permanent organizations, to appoint a greater number of officers. These usually are as follows :

PRESIDENT.
VICE-PRESIDENT.
SECRETARY.
CHAPLAIN.
HERALD.
CONDUCTOR.
MASTER OF CEREMONIES.
GUARD.

The collar and apron are the same as those of the Royal Arch degree.

No jewel until lately has been appropriated exclusively to this order. But in 1856, at a very general but informal meeting of Past High Priests, held at Hartford, during the session of the General Grand Chapter of the United States, the following jewel was unanimously adopted to designate those who had been anointed into the order of the High Priesthood :

8*

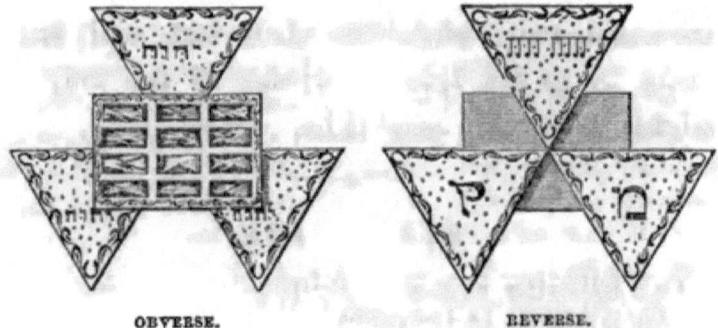

OBVERSE.   REVERSE.

It consists of a plate of gold in the form of a triple triangle, a breast-plate being placed over the point of union.
In front the face of each triangle is inscribed with the tetragrammaton, יְהוָֹה; on the other side the upper triangle has
the following mystical notation, ●●●● ●●●●● ; the two
lower triangles have the Hebrew letters מ and ק inserted
upon them. Each side of each triangle should be one inch
in length, and may be ornamented at the fancy of the wearer.
The breast-plate may be plainly engraved or set with stones.

Candidates receiving this order are said to be "anointed
into the holy order of the High Priesthood."

The following prayer may be used on opening a Convention:

PRAYER.

Oh, thou Supreme High Priest of Heaven and
earth, enlighten us, we beseech thee, with the knowledge of thy truth, and grant that the members of
this Convention, and all others who are teachers in
Israel, may be endowed with wisdom to understand
and to explain the mysteries of our order. Be with
us in all our assemblies, guide us in the paths of rectitude, and enable us to keep all thy statutes and

commandments, while life shall last, and finally bring us to the true knowledge of thy holy and mighty name. So mote it be. Amen.

RECEPTION.

THE following passage of Scripture is made use of during the ceremony of reception :

GENESIS xiv. 12–17.

And they took Lot, Abram's brother's son, (who dwelt in Sodom,) and his goods, and departed. And there came one that had escaped, and told Abram, the Hebrew; for he dwelt in the plain of Mamre, the Amorite, brother of Eschol, and brother of Aner ; and these were confederate with Abram. And when Abram heard that his brother was taken captive, he armed his trained servants, born in his own house, three hundred and eighteen, and pursued them unto Dan. And he divided himself against them, he and his servants, by night, and smote them, and pursued them unto Hobah, which is on the left hand of Damascus. And he brought back all the goods, and also brought again his brother Lot, and his goods, and the women also, and the people. And the king of Sodom went out to meet him, (after his return from the slaughter of Chedorlaomer, and of the kings that were with him,) at the valley of Sheveh, which is the king's dale.

The preceding verses of the chapter should also, be read as necessary to an understanding of certain portions of the investiture. They recount how *four* kings of Assyria, under the leadership of *Chedorlaomer*, king of Elam, attacked *five* kings living in the vale of Siddim, and having defeated them, took also Lot as their captive. "And there went out the king of Sodom and the king of Gomorrah, and the king of Admah, and the king of Zeboiim, and the king of Bela, (the same is Zoar) and they joined battle with them in the vale of Siddim; with Chedorlaomer the king of Elam, and with Tidal king of nations, and Amraphel king of Shinar, and Arioch king of Ellasar; *four kings with five.*"—GEN. xiv. 8, 9.

The following passage of Scripture should be read at this time:

GENESIS xiv. 18-24.

And Melchizedek, king of Salem, brought forth bread and wine: and he was the priest of the most high God. And he blessed him, and said, Blessed be Abram of the most high God, possessor of heaven and earth. And blessed be the most high God which hath delivered thine enemies into thy hand. And he gave him tithes of all. And the king of Sodom said unto Abram, Give me the persons and take the goods unto thyself. And Abram said unto the king of Sodom, I have lifted up my hand unto the Lord, the most high God, the possessor of heaven and earth, that I will not take from a thread even to a shoe latchet, and that I will not take any thing that is thine, lest thou shouldest say I have made Abram rich, save only that which the young men

have eaten, and the portion of the men which went
with me, Aner, Eschol and Mamre ; let them take
their portion.

THE COMMUNION OF BRETHREN.

IT was in ancient times a custom religiously observed, that
those who sacrificed to the gods, should unite in partaking
of a part of the food that had been offered. And in the
Jewish church it was strictly commanded that the sacrificer
should "eat before the Lord," and unite in a feast of joy on
the occasion of their offerings. By this common partaking
of that which had been consecrated to a sacred purpose,
those who **partook** of the feast seemed **to** give an evidence
and attestation of the sincerity with which they made the
offering, while the feast itself was, as it were, the renewal
of the covenant of friendship between the parties.

The anointment of a High Priest is preceded by the
following

PRAYER.

Most glorious and eternal High Priest of heaven
and earth, in thy mercy strengthen the works of our
hands, and grant that we may appear before thy
everlasting throne as pure and undefiled, as when
we descended from the loins of our father Abraham,
thy well beloved. Give us, O most merciful Lord,
an abundance of thy divine aid, so that we may be
embraced in his bosom in thy heavenly realms.
Pour down thy divine blessings on this, thy servant,
who is now kneeling before thee, with thy divine

glory, that he may vanquish and overcome all his enemies. Make him a true and faithful teacher of the companions over whom he has been chosen to preside, and enable him to perform the duties of his exalted office with fidelity and zeal, and we will praise thee, the Great I AM, forever and ever. So mote it be. Amen.

From a thread to a shoe latchet.

This was a proverbial expression, which ADAM CLARKE thus explains: Among the Rabbinical writers *chut* signifies a fillet worn by young women to tie up their hair. As Abram had taken both men and women captives, he says, " I have vowed that I will not receive the smallest portion of the property either of the women or of the men, from a girl's fillet to a man's shoe latchet."

In the same spirit the expression is used in this degree to denote the obligation of a High Priest never to wrong his companion even in so slight a matter as might be represented by these trifling articles of dress.

The Penalty for unlawfully assuming the Priesthood.

While MOSES was journeying through the wilderness, KORAH, DATHAN and ABIRAM were moved with envy and jealousy, that the priestly office had been restricted to AARON and his descendants. They accordingly appeared before MOSES, accompanied by a numerous band of conspirators, and demanded that the restriction should be removed, and they also be permitted to assume the priesthood. MOSES, shocked at their audacity, determined to leave the matter with the Lord, and therefore summoned them to appear the next day before the tabernacle with their censers, when he assured them that the Lord would show whom he had consecrated to these holy functions. On the next day, as KORAH, DATHAN and ABIRAM were about to burn incense before the tabernacle, the earth opened and they were swallowed up as a just punishment for unlawfully assuming the priesthood. The account is contained in the 16th chapter of the Book of Numbers, from verse 1 to 35, and is sometimes read in explanation of an important part of the investiture.

BENEDICTION.

When a High Priest is anointed, the following benediction **should** be recited:

NUMBERS vi. 22-26.

And the Lord spake unto Moses, saying, Speak unto Aaron and unto his sons, saying, On this wise ye shall bless the children of Israel, saying unto them, The Lord bless thee, and keep thee; the Lord make his face shine upon thee, and be gracious unto thee; the Lord lift up his countenance upon thee, and give thee peace.

The ceremony of anointing with oil preparatory to the assumption of any sacred office, as that of king or priest, was practised **both** among the Egyptians and the Jews. Among the monuments of the former, many representations are to be seen of the performance of this holy rite. The Scriptures mention three instances particularly in which unction was administered; namely, in the case of Aaron on his introduction into the priestly office, and of David and Solomon at their consecration as kings. The anointing was in all these cases viewed as a symbol of sanctification, of a designation to the service of God, or to a holy and sacred use.

The following passage of Scripture is read as explanatory of the office of the priesthood. It may be very appropriately used as a concluding charge:

HEBREWS vii. 1–6.

For this Melchizedek, king of Salem, priest of the Most High God, (who met Abraham returning from the slaughter of the kings, and blessed him; to whom also Abraham gave a tenth part of all; first being, by interpretation, King of Righteousness, and after that also King of Salem, which is, King of Peace; without father, without mother, without descent; having neither beginning of days, nor end of life; but made like unto the Son of God,) abideth a priest continually. Now consider how great this man was, unto whom even the patriarch Abraham gave the tenth of the spoils. And verily, they that are of the sons of Levi, who receive the office of the priesthood, have a commandment to take tithes of the people, according to the law, that is of their brethren, though they come out of the loins of Abraham. For he testifieth, Thou art a priest for ever, after the order of Melchizedek. And inasmuch as not without an oath, he was made priest. For those priests (under the Levitical law) were made without an oath; but this with an oath, by him that said unto him, The Lord sware, and will not repent, Thou art a priest for ever, after the order of Melchizedek.

END OF THE ORDER OF HIGH PRIESTHOOD.

BOOK VI.

Ceremonies of the Order.

" On the most ordinary occasions, forms and ceremonies are bene-
ficial; on important occasions they become necessary; and most
surely those persons are not wise who regard them with indifference,
much more those who regard them with contempt."

DUDLEY'S NAOLOGY.

CEREMONIES OF THE ORDER.

SECTION I.

CONSECRATION OF A NEW CHAPTER.

Thu new Chapter will meet in its hall, and open on the Royal Arch degree; the Grand Officers will meet in an adjoining room, and on being notified by a committee of the new Chapter that its members are ready for their reception, they will proceed to the Chapter room, where being received by the new Chapter with the Grand Honors, the officers of the new Chapter resign their stations to the Grand officers. A procession is then formed by the Grand Captain of the Host, as follows, which repairs to the church, or place designated for the performance of the ceremonies.

Sentinel.
Mark Masters, by twos.
Past Masters, by twos.
Most Excellent Masters, by twos.
Royal Arch Masons, triangularly, two in front and one behind.
Members of the new Chapter, triangularly.
Masters of the First and Second Veil,
Masters of the Third Veil.
Royal Arch Captain, Principal Sojourner.
Captain of the Host.
Secretary and Treasurer.
One Companion carrying the Pot of Incense.
Four Companions carrying the Ark.
Three Companions carrying lights, triangularly.
Scribe and King.

(187)

High Priest.
Grand Sentinel.
Members of the Grand Chapter, triangularly.
Grand Royal Arch Captain.
Grand Secretary and Grand Treasurer.
Grand Chaplain, Orator.
Deputy Grand High Priest.
Grand Scribe, Grand King.
Grand High Priest.

On arriving at the church, or place where the ceremonies are to be performed, the procession halts, faces inwards, and the Grand officers and others pass through. All being seated, the ceremonies commence as follows:

ANTHEM.

PRAYER BY THE GRAND CHAPLAIN.

Almighty and Supreme High Priest of Heaven and Earth! Who is there in heaven but thee! and who upon earth can stand in competition with thee! Thy OMNISCIENT Mind brings all things in review, past, present, and to come; thine OMNIPOTENT Arm directs the movements of the vast creation; thine OMNIPRESENT Eye pervades the secret recesses of every heart; thy boundless beneficence supplies us with every comfort and enjoyment; and thine unspeakable perfections and glory surpass the understanding of the children of men! Our Father, who art in heaven, we invoke thy benediction upon the purposes of our present assembly. May this Chapter be established to thine honor, and consecrated to thy glory; may its officers be endowed with wisdom to discern, and fidelity to pursue, its true interests ; and may its members be ever mindful of the duty they owe to their God, the obedience they owe to their superiors, the love they owe to their equals, and the good will they owe to all mankind.

Glory be to God on high.

Response. As it was in the beginning, is now, and ever shall be, world without end. So mote it be. Amen.

ORATION.

The Grand Captain of the Host then forms the new Chapter in front of the Grand High Priest.

The Deputy Grand High Priest says :

Most Excellent Grand High Priest, a number of Companions, duly instructed in the sublime mysteries, being desirous of promoting the honor, and propagating the principles of the Art, have applied to the Grand Chapter for a Warrant to constitute a new Chapter of Royal Arch Masons, which having been obtained, they are now assembled for the purpose of being constituted, and having their officers installed in due and ancient form.

GRAND HIGH PRIEST. Let the Warrant of Constitution be read.

GRAND SECRETARY reads it.

GRAND HIGH PRIEST. Companions, do you still approve of the officers as named herein ?

COMPANIONS. We do.

GRAND HIGH PRIEST. By virtue of the high powers in me vested, I do form you, my respected Companions, into a regular Chapter of Royal Arch Masons. From henceforth you are authorized and empowered to open and hold a Lodge of Mark Masters, Past Masters, and Most Excellent Masters, and a Chapter of Royal Arch Masons; and to do and perform all such things as thereunto may appertain; conforming in all your doings to *the General Grand Royal Arch Constitution, and** the general regulations of the State Grand Chapter. And may the God of your fathers be with you, guide, and direct you in all your doings.

The Ark of the Covenant, and the furniture, clothing, jewels, and implements belonging to the Chapter, (having been previously placed in the centre, in front of the Grand High Priest,) are now uncovered, and the dedication proceeds.

The Grand Chaplain, with the pot of incense in his hands, says:

To our most excellent patron Zerubbabel, we solemnly dedicate this Chapter. May the blessing of our Heavenly High Priest descend and rest upon its members, and may their felicity be immortal. Glory be to God on High.

Response. As it was in the beginning, is now, and ever shall be, world without end. Amen.

---

* These words marked in italics and the same words similarly designated in other parts of these services may be omitted in those States which are not under the jurisdiction of the General Grand Chapter.

Music, or an Ode.

The Deputy Grand High Priest then presents the High Priest of the new Chapter to the Grand High Priest, saying:

Most Excellent Grand High Priest, I present you Companion . . . . . . , nominated in the Warrant, to be installed **High Priest** of this new Chapter. I find him to be skillful in the royal art, and attentive to the moral precepts of our forefathers, and have therefore no doubt but he will discharge the duties of his office with fidelity.

The Grand High Priest then addresses him as follows:

Most Excellent: I feel much satisfaction in performing my duty on the present occasion, by installing you into the office of High Priest of this Chapter. It is an office highly honorable to all those who diligently perform the important duties annexed to it. Your reputed Masonic knowledge, however, precludes the necessity of a particular enumeration of those duties. I shall therefore only observe, that by a frequent recurrence to the constitution, and general regulations, and the constant study of our sublime science, you will be best able to fulfill them; and I am confident that the Companions who are chosen to preside with you, will give strength to your endeavors, and support to your exertions. I shall now propose certain questions to you, relative to the duties of your office, to which I must request your unequivocal answer

1. Do you solemnly promise that you will re-double your endeavors to correct the vices, purify the morals, and promote the happiness of those of your Companions, who have **attained this sublime** degree?

2. That you will never suffer your chapter to be opened, unless there be present nine regular Royal Arch Masons?

3. That you will never suffer either more or less than three brethren to be exalted in your Chapter at one and the same time?

4. That you will not exalt any one to this degree who has not shown a charitable and humane dispo-sition; or who has not made a considerable pro-ficiency in the foregoing degrees?

5. That you will promote the general good of our order, and, on all proper occasions, be ready to give and receive instructions, particularly from the *General and* State Grand officers?

6. That, to the utmost of your power, you will preserve the solemnities of our ceremonies, and behave, in open Chapter, with the most profound respect and reverence, as an example to your Com-panions?

7. That you will not acknowledge, or have **inter-**course with any Chapter that does not work **under a** constitutional warrant or dispensation?

8. That you will not admit any visitor into your Chapter, who has not been exalted in a Chapter legally constituted, without his being first formally healed?

9. That you will observe and support such by-laws as may be made by your Chapter, in conformity to *the General Grand Royal Arch Constitution, and* the general regulations of the Grand Chapter?

10. That you will pay respect and due obedience to the instructions of the *General and* State Grand Officers, particularly relating to the several Lectures and Charges, and will resign the chair to them, severally, when they may visit your Chapter?

11. That you will support and observe *the General Grand Royal Arch Constitution, and* the General Regulations of the Grand Royal Arch Chapter, under whose authority you act?

Do you submit to all these things, and do you promise to observe and practice them faithfully?

Answer. I do.

All then kneel, and the Grand Chaplain offers the following

PRAYER.

Most holy and glorious Lord God, the Great High Priest of Heaven and Earth;

We approach thee with reverence, and implore thy blessing on the Companion appointed to preside

9

over this new assembly, and now prostrate before
thee ;—fill his heart with thy fear, that his tongue
and actions may pronounce thy glory. Make him
steadfast in thy service; grant him firmness of mind ;
animate his heart, and strengthen his endeavors;
may he teach thy judgments and thy laws; and may
the incense he shall put before thee, upon thine
altar, prove an acceptable sacrifice unto thee. Bless
him, O Lord, and bless the work of his hands.
Accept us in mercy ; hear thou from heaven thy
dwelling-place, and forgive our transgressions.

Glory be to God on high.

Response. As it was in the beginning, is now,
and ever shall be, world without end. So mote it
be. Amen.

The Grand High Priest then administers the following
obligation to the High Priest:

I, ... , do promise and swear that I will
serve this Chapter as High Priest for the time that
I have been elected : that I will perform all the
duties appertaining to that office to the best of my
abilities, and will support and maintain the Constitution of the Grand Chapter of . . . . , *and that of
the General Grand Chapter of the United States.*"

The Grand High Priest will then cause the High Priest
to be invested with the clothing and badges of his office,
and address him as follows:

MOST EXCELLENT : In consequence of your cheerful acquiescence with the charges which you have heard recited, you are qualified for installation as the High Priest of this Royal Arch Chapter ; and it is incumbent upon me, on this occasion, to point out some of the particulars appertaining to your office, duty, and dignity.

The High Priest of every Chapter has it in special charge, to see that the by-laws of his Chapter, *as well as the General Grand Royal Arch Constitution*, and all the regulations of the Grand Chapter, are duly observed ;—that all the officers of his Chapter perform the duties of their respective offices faithfully, and are examples of diligence and industry to their Companions ;—that true and accurate records of all the proceedings of the Chapter are kept by the Secretary ;—that the Treasurer keeps and renders exact and just accounts of all the moneys and other property belonging to the Chapter ;—that the regular returns be made annually to the Grand Chapter ;—and that the annual dues to the Grand Chapter be regularly and punctually paid. He has the right and authority of calling his Chapter together at pleasure, upon any emergency or occurrence, which in his judgment may require their meeting. It is his privilege and duty, together with the King and Scribe, to attend the meetings of the Grand Chapter, either in person or by proxy ; and the well-being of the institution requires that this duty should on no occasion be omitted.

The office of High Priest is a station highly honorable to all those who diligently perform the important duties annexed to it. By a frequent recurrence to the constitutions and general regulations, and a constant practice of the several sublime Lectures and Charges, you will be best enabled to fulfill those duties ; and I am confident that the Companions who are chosen to preside with **you**, will give strength to your endeavors, and support to your exertions.

Let the *Mitre* with which you are invested, remind you of the dignity of the office you sustain, and its inscription impress upon your mind a sense of your dependence upon God ;—that perfection is not given unto man upon earth, and that perfect holiness belongeth alone unto the Lord.

The *Breast-Plate*, with which you are decorated, in imitation of that upon which were engraven the names of the twelve tribes, and worn by the High Priest of Israel, is to teach you that you are always to bear in mind your responsibility to the laws and ordinances of the institution, and that the honor and interests of your Chapter and its members, should be always near your heart.

The *various colors* of the *Robes* you wear, are emblematical of every grace and virtue which can adorn and beautify the human mind ; each of which will be briefly illustrated in the course of the charges to be delivered to your subordinate officers.

You will now take charge of your officers, standing upon their right, and present them severally in succession to the Deputy Grand High Priest, by whom they will be presented to me for installation.

The High Priest of the Chapter will then present each of his officers in succession to the Deputy Grand High Priest, who will present the officer to the Grand High Priest, in the words already used in presenting the High Priest, as printed on page 191, making the necessary variation for the office. The Grand High Priest will administer an obligation similar to that administered to the High Priest, and after investing each officer with his clothing and badges, he will address him as follows :

CHARGE TO THE KING.

EXCELLENT COMPANION : The important station to which you are elected in this Chapter, requires from you exemplary conduct; its duties demand your most assiduous attention ; you are to second and support your chief in all the requirements of his office ; and should casualties at any time prevent his attendance, you are to succeed him in the performance of his duties.

Your badge *(the Level surmounted by a Crown)* should remind you that although you are the repre-

sentative of a King, and exalted by office above your
Companions, yet that you remain upon a level with
them, as respects your duty to God, to your neighbor, and to yourself; that you are equally bound
with them, to be obedient to the laws and ordinances of the institution; to be charitable, humane,
and just, and to seek every occasion of doing good.

Your office teaches a striking lesson of humility.
The institutions of political society teach us to consider the king as the chief of created beings, and
that the first duty of his subjects is to obey his mandates :—but the institutions of our sublime degrees,
by placing the King in a situation subordinate to
the High Priest, teach us that our duty to God is
paramount to all other duties, and should ever claim
the priority of our obedience to man; and that however strongly we may be bound to obey the laws of
civil society, yet that those laws, to be just, should
never intermeddle with matters of conscience, nor
dictate articles of faith.

The *Scarlet Robe*, an emblem of imperial dignity,
should remind you of the paternal concern you
should ever feel for the welfare of your Chapter,
and the *fervency* and *zeal* with which you should
endeavor to promote its prosperity.

In presenting to you the *Crown*, which is an emblem of royalty, I would remind you, that to reign

sovereign in the hearts and affections of men, must be far more grateful to a generous and benevolent mind, than to rule over their lives and fortunes; and that to enable you to enjoy this pre-eminence with honor and satisfaction, you must subject your own passions and prejudices to the dominion of reason and charity.

You are entitled to the second seat in the council of your Companions. Let the bright example of your illustrious predecessor in the Grand Council at Jerusalem, stimulate you to the faithful discharge of your duties; and when the King of Kings shall summon you into his immediate presence, from his hand may you receive a *crown of glory*, which shall never fade away.

CHARGE TO THE SCRIBE.

EXCELLENT COMPANION: The office of Scribe, to which you are elected, is very important and respectable. In the absence of your superior officers, you are bound to succeed them, and to perform their duties. The purposes of the institution ought never to suffer for want of intelligence in its proper officers; you will therefore perceive the necessity there is of your possessing such qualifications as will enable you to accomplish those duties which are incumbent upon you, in your appropriate station, as well as those which may occasionally de-volve upon you by the absence of your superiors.

The *Purple Robe*, with which you are invested, is an emblem of *union*, and is calculated to remind you that the harmony and unanimity of the Chapter should be your constant aim; and to this end you are studiously to avoid all occasions of giving offence, or countenancing anything that may create divisions or dissensions. You are, by all means in your power, to endeavor to establish a permanent union and good understanding among all orders and degrees of masonry, and as the glorious sun, at its meridian height, dispels the mist and clouds which obscure the horizon, so may your exertions tend to dissipate the gloom of jealousy and discord, when-ever they may appear.

Your badge *(a Plum-rule surmounted by the Tur-ban)* is an emblem of rectitude and vigilance; and while you stand as a watchman on the tower, to guard your Companions against the approach of those enemies of human felicity, *intemperance* and *excess*, let this faithful monitor ever remind you to walk uprightly in your station; admonishing and animating your Companions to fidelity and industry while at labor, and to temperance and moderation while at refreshment. And when the Great Watch-man of Israel, whose eye never slumbers or sleeps, shall relieve you from your post on earth, may he permit you in heaven to participate in that food and refreshment which is

"Such as the saints in glory love,
And such as the angels eat."

CHARGE TO THE CAPTAIN OF THE HOST.

COMPANION : The office with which you are entrusted is of high importance, and demands your most zealous consideration. The preservation of the most essential traits of our ancient customs, usages, and landmarks, are within your province ; and it is indispensably necessary that the part assigned to you, in the immediate practice of our rites and ceremonies, should be perfectly understood, and correctly administered.

Your office corresponds with that of Marshal, or Master of Ceremonies. You are to superintend all processions of your Chapter, when moving as a distinct body, either in public or private ; and as the world can only judge of our private discipline by our public deportment, you will be careful that the utmost order and decorum be observed on all such occasions. You will ever be attentive to the commands of your chief, and always near at hand to see them duly executed. I invest you with the badge of your office, and presume that you will give to your duties all that study and attention which their importance demands.

9*

CHARGE TO THE PRINCIPAL SOJOURNER.

COMPANION : The office confided to you, though subordinate in degree, is equal in importance to any in the Chapter, that of your chief alone excepted. Your office corresponds with that of *Senior Deacon*, in the preparatory degrees. Among the duties required of you, the preparation and introduction of candidates are not the least. As in our intercourse with the world, experience teaches that first impressions are often the most durable, and the most difficult to eradicate ; so it is of great importance, in all cases, that those impressions should be correct and just ; hence it is essential that the officer, who brings the blind by a way they knew not, and leads them in paths that they have not known, should always be well qualified to make darkness **light before** them, and crooked things straight.

Your *robe of office* is an emblem of humility ; and teaches that in the prosecution of a laudable undertaking, we should never decline taking any part that **may** be assigned us, although it may be the most difficult or dangerous.

The *rose-colored tesselated Border*, adorning the robe, is an emblem of ardor and perseverance, and signifies that when we have engaged in a virtuous course, notwithstanding all the impediments, hardships, **and** trials, we may be destined to encounter, we should endure them all with fortitude, and ardently persevere unto the end; resting assured of receiving, at the termination of our labors, a noble and glorious reward. Your past exertions will be considered as a pledge of your future assiduity in the faithful discharge of your duties.

CHARGE TO THE ROYAL ARCH CAPTAIN.

COMPANION: The well-known duties of your station require but little elucidation. Your office in the preparatory degrees corresponds with that of *Junior Deacon*. It is your province, conjointly with the Captain of the Host, to attend the examination of all visitors, and to take care that none are permitted to enter the Chapter, but such as have *traveled the rugged path* of trial, and evinced their title to our favor and friendship. You will be attentive to obey the commands of the Captain of the Host during *the introduction of strangers among* the workmen; so that should they be permitted to pass your post, they may by him be introduced into the presence of the Grand Council.

The *White Banner*, entrusted to your care, is emblematical of that purity of heart and rectitude of conduct, which ought to actuate all those who pass the white veil of the sanctuary. I give it to you strongly in charge, never to suffer any one to pass your post, without the *signet of truth*.

I present you the badge of your office, in expectation of your performing your duties with intelligence, assiduity, and propriety.

CHARGE TO THE GRAND MASTER OF THE THIRD VEIL.

COMPANION : I present you with the *Scarlet Banner*, which is the ensign of your office, and with a sword to protect and defend the same. The rich and beautiful color of your banner is emblematical of *fervency* and *zeal;* it is the appropriate color of the Royal Arch degree ; it admonishes us, that we should be fervent in the exercise of our devotions to God, and zealous in our endeavors to promote the happiness of man.

CHARGE TO THE GRAND MASTER OF THE SECOND VEIL.

COMPANION : I invest you with the *Purple Banner*, which is the ensign of your office, and arm you with a sword, to enable you to maintain its honor.

The color of your banner is produced by a due mixture of *blue* and *scarlet;* the former of which is the characteristic color of the *symbolic* or *first three degrees of masonry*, and the latter, that of the *Royal Arch degree*. It is an emblem of *union*, and is the characteristic color of the intermediate degrees. It admonishes us to cultivate and improve that spirit of union and harmony, between the brethren of the symbolic degrees and the Companions of the sublime degrees, which should ever distinguish the members of a society founded upon the principles of everlasting truth and universal philanthropy.

CHARGE TO THE GRAND MASTER OF THE FIRST VEIL.

COMPANION : I invest you with the *Blue Banner*, which is the ensign of your office, and a sword for its defence and protection. The color of your banner is one of the most durable and beautiful in nature. It is the appropriate color adopted and worn by our ancient brethren of the three symbolic degrees, and is the *peculiar characteristic* of an institution which has stood the test of ages, and which is as much distinguished by the durability of its materials or principles, as by the beauty of its superstructure. It is an emblem of universal *friendship* and *benevolence ;* and instructs us, that in the mind of a mason, those virtues should be as expansive as the blue arch of heaven itself.

CHARGE TO THE TREASURER.

COMPANION : You are elected Treasurer of this Chapter, and I have the pleasure of investing you with the badge of your office. The qualities which should recommend a Treasurer are *accuracy* and *fidelity;* accuracy, in keeping a fair and minute account of all receipts and disbursements ; fidelity, in carefully preserving all the property and funds of the Chapter, that may be placed in his hands, and rendering a just account of the same whenever he is called upon for that purpose. I presume that your respect for the institution, your attachment to the interests of your Chapter, and your regard for a good name, which is better than precious ointment, will prompt you to the faithful discharge of the duties of your office.

CHARGE TO THE SECRETARY.

COMPANION: I with pleasure invest you with your badge as Secretary of this Chapter. The qualities which should recommend a Secretary, are, *promptitude* in issuing the notifications and orders of his superior officers; *punctuality* in attending the convocations of the Chapter; *correctness* in recording their proceedings; *judgment* in discriminating between what is proper and what is improper to be committed to writing; *regularity* in making his annual returns to the Grand Chapter; *integrity* in accounting for all moneys that may pass through his hands; and *fidelity* in paying the same over into the hands of the Treasurer. The possession of these good qualities, I presume, has designated you as a suitable candidate for this important office; and I cannot entertain a doubt that you will discharge its duties beneficially to the Chapter, and honorably to yourself. And when you shall have completed the record of your transactions here below, and finished the term of your probation, may you be admitted

into the celestial Grand Chapter of saints and angels, and find your name *recorded* in the *book of life
eternal.*

CHARGE TO THE SENTINEL.

COMPANION : You are appointed Sentinel of this
Chapter ; and I invest you with the badge, and this
implement of your office. As the sword is placed in
the hands of the Sentinel, to enable him effectually
to guard against the approach of all *cowans and
eavesdroppers,* and suffer none to pass or repass but
such as are *duly qualified ;* so it should morally serve
as a constant admonition to us to set a guard at the
entrance of our thoughts ; to place a watch at the
door of our lips ; to post a sentinel at the avenue
of our actions ; thereby excluding every unqualified
and unworthy thought, word and deed ; and preserving consciences void of offence towards God and
towards man.

As the first application from visitors for admission into the Chapter is generally made to the Sentinel at the door, your station will often present you
to the observation of strangers ; it is, therefore,
essentially necessary that he who sustains the office
with which you are entrusted, should be a man of
good morals, steady habits, strict discipline, temperate, affable and discreet. I trust that a just regard
for the honor and reputation of the institution, will

ever induce you to perform with fidelity the trust reposed in you ; and when the door of this earthly tabernacle shall be closed, may you find an abundant entrance through the gates into the temple and city of our God.

The Grand High Priest then delivers the following

CHARGE TO THE CHAPTER.

COMPANIONS : The exercise and management of the sublime degrees of masonry in your Chapter hitherto, are so highly appreciated, and the good reputation of the Chapter so well established, that I must presume these considerations alone, were there no others of greater magnitude, would be sufficient to induce you to preserve and perpetuate this valuable and honorable character.   But when to these is added the pleasure which every philanthropic heart must feel in doing good, in promoting good order, in diffusing light and knowledge, in cultivating masonic and Christian charity, which are the great objects of this sublime institution, I cannot doubt that your future conduct, and that of your successors, will be calculated still to increase the lustre of your justly esteemed reputation.

May your *chapter* become *beautiful* as the *temple*, *peaceful* as the *ark*, and *sacred* as its *most holy place*. May your oblations of *piety* and *praise* be *grateful* as the *incense*, your love *warm* as its *flame*, and your charity diffusive as its fragrance. May your hearts be *pure* as the *altar*, and your conduct *acceptable* as the *offering*. May the exercises of your *charity* be as constant as the returning wants of the distressed *widow* and helpless *orphan*. May the approbation of Heaven be your encouragement, and the testimony of a good conscience your support: may you be endowed with every good and perfect gift, while *traveling* the *rugged path* of life, and finally be *admitted within the veil* of heaven, to the full enjoyment of life eternal. So mote it be. Amen.

The officers and members of the Chapter will then pass in review in front of the Grand officers, with their hands crossed on their breasts, bowing as they pass.

The Grand Captain of the Host then makes the following proclamation:

"In the name of the Most Excellent Grand Chapter of the State of . . . . . , I hereby proclaim . . . . Chapter No. . . . , to be legally constituted and consecrated, and the officers thereof duly installed, with the Grand Honors of Masonry, by three times three."

The public Grand Honors are then given.

An Ode.

Benediction by the Grand Chaplain.

The procession then returns to the Chapter room, and the Grand officers retiring, the Chapter is closed by its own officers.

ANNUAL INSTALLATION OF THE OFFICERS
OF A CHAPTER.

On the night appointed for the installation, the Chapter being opened in the Royal Arch Degree, a Past High Priest, if one be present, and if not, some other officer presents the High Priest elect to the Presiding officer, and says:

Most Excellent: I hereby present before you Companion . . . . . . , who has been duly elected to serve this Chapter as High Priest for the ensuing masonic year, and who now declares himself ready for installation.

The High Priest elect then turning and facing the Companions, the Presiding officer says:

Companions: You now behold before you Companion . . . . . . , who has been elected to serve this Chapter as Most Excellent High Priest, and who now declares himself ready for installation. If any of you have any reasons to urge why he should not be installed, you will make them known now, or else forever hereafter hold your peace. Hearing no objections, I shall proceed to install him.

The Presiding officer then addresses him as follows:

Most Excellent: I feel much satisfaction in performing my duty on the present occasion, by installing you into the office of High Priest of this Chapter. It is an office highly honorable to all those who diligently perform the important duties annexed to it. Your reputed Masonic knowledge, however, precludes the necessity of a particular enumeration of those duties. I shall therefore only observe, that by a frequent recurrence to the constitution, and general regulations, and constant practice of the several sublime lectures and charges, you will best be able to fulfill them; and I am confident that the Companions who are chosen to preside with you, will give strength to your endeavors, and support to your exertions. I shall now propose certain questions to you, relative to the duties of your office, to which I must request your unequivocal answer.

1. Do you solemnly promise that you will redouble your endeavors to correct the vices, purify the morals, and promote the happiness of those of your Companions, who have attained this sublime degree?

2. That you will never suffer your chapter to be opened, unless there be present nine regular Royal Arch Masons?

3. That you will never suffer either more or less than three brethren to be exalted in your Chapter at one and the same time?

4. That you will not exalt any one to this degree

who has not shown a charitable and humane disposition; or who has not made a considerable proficiency in the foregoing degrees?

5. That you will promote the general **good of our** order, and, on all proper occasions, be ready to give and receive instructions, particularly from the *General and* State Grand officers?

6. That, to the utmost of your power, you will preserve the solemnities of our ceremonies, and behave, in open Chapter, with the most profound respect and reverence, as an example to your Companions?

7. That you will not acknowledge, or have intercourse with any Chapter that does not work under a constitutional warrant or dispensation?

8. That you will not admit any visitor into your Chapter, who has not been exalted **in a** Chapter legally constituted, without his being **first formally** healed?

9. That you will observe and support such by-laws as may be made by your Chapter, in conformity to *the General Grand Royal Arch Constitution,* **and** the general regulations of the Grand Chapter?

10. **That you will pay respect** and due obedience to the instructions of the *General and* State Grand Officers, particularly relating to the several Lectures and Charges, and will resign the chair to them, severally, when they may visit your Chapter?

11. That you will support and observe *the General Grand Royal Arch Constitution, and* the General Regulations of the Grand Royal Arch Chapter, under whose authority you act?

Do you submit to all these things, and do you promise to observe and practice them faithfully?

Answer. I do.

All then kneel, and the Grand Chaplain offers the following

PRAYER.

Most holy and glorious Lord God, the Great High Priest of Heaven and Earth;

We approach thee with reverence, and implore thy blessing on the Companion appointed to preside over this Chapter, and now prostrate before thee; —fill his heart with thy fear, that his tongue and actions may pronounce thy glory. Make him steadfast in thy service; grant him firmness of mind; animate his heart, and strengthen his endeavors; may he teach thy judgments and thy laws; and may the incense he shall put before thee, upon thine altar, prove an acceptable sacrifice unto thee. Bless him, O Lord, and bless the work of his hands. Accept us in mercy; hear thou from heaven thy dwelling-place, and forgive our transgressions

Glory be to God on high.

Response. As it was in the beginning, is now,

and ever shall be, world without end. So mote it be. Amen.

The Presiding officer then administers the following obligation to the High Priest elect:

I, ... , do promise and swear that I will serve this Chapter as High Priest for the time that I have been elected: that I will perform all the duties appertaining to that office to the best of my abilities, and will support and maintain the Constitution of the Grand Chapter of . . . . , *and that of the General Grand Chapter of the United States."*

The Grand High Priest will then cause the High Priest to be invested with the clothing and badges of his office, and will address him as follows:

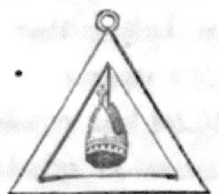 MOST EXCELLENT: In consequence of your cheerful acquiescence with the charges which you have heard recited, you are qualified for installation as the High Priest of this Royal Arch Chapter; and it is incumbent upon me, on this occasion, to point out some of the particulars appertaining to your office, duty, and dignity.

The High Priest of every Chapter has it in special charge, to see that the by-laws of his Chapter, *as well as the General Grand Royal Arch Constitution,* and all the regulations of the Grand Chapter, are duly observed;—that all the officers of his Chapter perform the duties of their respective offices faithfully, and are examples of diligence and industry to their Companions ;—that true and accurate records of all the proceedings of the Chapter are kept by the Secretary ;—that the Treasurer keeps and renders exact and just accounts of all the moneys and other property belonging to the Chapter ;—that the regular returns be made annually to the Grand Chapter ;—and that the annual dues to the Grand Chapter be regularly and punctually paid. He has the right and authority of calling his Chapter together at pleasure, upon any emergency or occurrence, which in his judgment may require their meeting. It is his privilege and duty, together with the King and Scribe, to attend the meetings of the Grand Chapter, either in person or by proxy ; and the well-being of the institution requires that this duty should on no occasion be omitted.

The office of High Priest is a station highly honorable to all those who diligently perform the important duties annexed to it. By a frequent recurrence to the constitutions and general regulations, and a constant practice of the several sublime Lectures and Charges, you will be best enabled to fulfill those duties ; and I am confident that the Companions who are chosen to preside with you, will give strength to your endeavors, and support to your exertions.

Let the *Mitre* with which you are invested, remind you of the dignity of the office you sustain, and its inscription impress upon your mind a sense of your dependence upon God;—that perfection is not given unto man upon earth, and that **perfect holiness** belongeth alone unto the Lord.

The *Breast-Plate*, with which you are decorated, in imitation of that upon which were engraven the names of the twelve tribes, and worn by the High Priest of Israel, is to teach you that you are always to bear in mind your responsibility to the laws and ordinances of the institution, and that the honor and interests of your Chapter and its **members, should** be always near your heart.

The *various colors* of the *Robes* you wear, **are** emblematical of every grace and virtue which **can** adorn and beautify the human mind ; each **of** which will be briefly illustrated in the course of the charges to be delivered to your subordinate officers.

You will own assume your seat in the *Sanctum Sanctorum*, and proceed to the installation of your subordinate officers.

The High Priest is then inducted into the *Sanctum Sanctorum*. Each of the subordinate officers is presented to him by the Past High Priest, with the same address as is recited above, and the same call is made in each case, for objections; the same obligation, (with the necessary variation of title,) which had been taken by the High Priest, is taken by each of the officers, and the charge is read to him by the High Priest elect, after which the newly installed officer assumes his appropriate station in the Chapter.

CHARGE TO THE KING.

EXCELLENT COMPANION : The important station to which you are elected in this Chapter, requires from you exemplary conduct ; its duties demand your most assiduous attention ; you are to second and support your chief in all the requirements of his office ; and should casualties at any time prevent his attendance, you are to succeed him in the performance of his duties.

Your badge (*the Level surmounted by a Crown*) should remind you that although you are the representative of a King, and exalted by office above your Companions, yet that you remain upon a level with them, as respects your duty to God, to your neighbor, and to yourself ; that you are equally bound with them, to be obedient to the laws and ordinances of the institution ; to be charitable, humane, and just, and to seek every occasion of doing good.

Your office teaches a striking lesson of humility. The institutions of political society teach us to consider the king as the chief of created beings, and that the first duty of his subjects is to obey his mandates :—but the institutions of our sublime degrees,

10

by placing the King in a situation subordinate to the High Priest, teach us that our duty to God is paramount to all other duties, and should ever claim the priority of our obedience to man ; and that however strongly we may be bound to obey the laws of civil society, yet that those laws, to be just, should never intermeddle with matters of conscience, nor dictate articles of faith.

The *Scarlet Robe*, an emblem of imperial dignity, should remind you of the paternal concern you should ever feel for the welfare of your Chapter, and the *fervency* and *zeal* with which you should endeavor to promote its prosperity.

In presenting to you the *Crown*, which is an emblem of royalty, I would remind you, that to reign sovereign in the hearts and affections of men, must be far more grateful to a generous and benevolent mind than to rule over their lives and fortunes ; and that to enable you to enjoy this pre-eminence with honor and satisfaction, you must subject your own passions and prejudices to the dominion of reason and charity.

You are entitled to the second seat in the council of your Companions. Let the bright example of your illustrious predecessor in the Grand Council at Jerusalem, stimulate you to the faithful discharge of your duties ; and when the King of Kings shall summon you into his immediate presence, from his

hand may you receive a *crown of glory*, which shall
never fade away.

CHARGE TO THE SCRIBE.

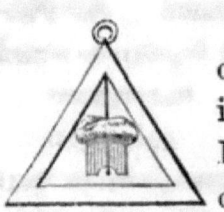 EXCELLENT COMPANION: The office
of Scribe, to which you are elected,
is very important and respectable.
In the absence of your superior officers, you are bound to succeed them,
and to perform their duties. The purposes of the
institution ought never to suffer for want of intelligence in its proper officers ; you will therefore perceive the necessity there is of your possessing such
qualifications as will enable you to accomplish those
duties which are incumbent upon you, in your appropriate station, as well as those which may occasionally devolve on you, by the absence of your
superiors.

The *Purple Robe*, with which you are invested, is
an emblem of *union*, and is calculated to remind you
that the harmony and unanimity of the Chapter
should be your constant aim ; and to this end you
are studiously to avoid all occasions of giving
offence, or countenancing anything that may create
divisions or dissensions. You are, by all means in
your power, to endeavor to establish a permanent
union and good understanding among all orders and
degrees of masonry ; and as the glorious sun, at its

meridian height, dispels the mist and clouds which obscure the horizon, so **may your** exertions tend to dissipate **the** gloom of jealousy and discord, whenever **they** may appear.

Your badge (*a Plumb-rule surmounted by the Turban*) is an emblem of rectitude and vigilance ; **and** while you stand as a watchman on the tower, to guard your Companions against the approach **of** those enemies of human felicity, *intemperance* and *excess*, **let** this faithful monitor ever remind you to **walk** uprightly in your station ; admonishing and animating your Companions to **fidelity and** industry while at labor, and to temperance **and** moderation while at refreshment.   And when the Great Watchman of Israel, whose eye never slumbers nor sleeps, shall relieve you from your **post on** earth, may he permit you in heaven to participate **in that** food and refreshment **which is**

> " Such as the saints in glory love,
> And such as angels eat."

CHARGE TO THE CAPTAIN OF THE HOST.

Companion : The office with which you are entrusted is of high importance, and demands your most zealous consideration.   The preservation of the **most** essential traits of our ancient customs, usages, and landmarks, are within your province ; and it is indispensably necessary, that the part assigned to you, in the immediate practice of our rites and ceremonies, should be perfectly understood, and correctly administered.

Your office corresponds with that of Marshal, or Master of Ceremonies. You are to superintend all processions of your Chapter, when moving as a distinct body, either in public or private; and as the world can only judge of our private discipline by our public deportment, you will be careful that the utmost order and decorum be observed on all such occasions. You will ever be attentive to the commands of your chief, and always near at hand to see them duly executed. I invest you with the badge of your office, and presume that you will give to your duties all that study and attention which their importance demands.

CHARGE TO THE PRINCIPAL SOJOURNER.

COMPANION: The office confided to you, though subordinate in degree, is equal in importance to any in the Chapter, that of your chief alone excepted. Your office corresponds with that of *Senior Deacon*, in the preparatory degrees. Among the duties required of you, the preparation and introduction of candidates are not the least. As in our intercourse with the world, experience teaches that first impressions are often

the most durable, and the most difficult to erad
icate; so it is of great importance, in all cases,
that those impressions should be correct and just;
hence it is essential that the officer, who brings the
blind by a way that they knew not, and leads them
in paths that they have not known, should always
be well qualified to make darkness light before
them, and crooked things straight.

Your *robe of office* is an emblem of humility; and
teaches that in the prosecution of a laudable undertaking, we should never decline taking any part that
may be assigned us, although it may be the most
difficult or dangerous.

The *rose-colored tesselated Border*, adorning the
robe, is an emblem of ardor and perseverance, and
signifies that when we have engaged in a virtuous
course, notwithstanding all the impediments, hardships, and trials, we may be destined to encounter,
we should endure them all with fortitude, and ardently persevere unto the end; resting assured of
receiving, at the termination of our labors, a noble
and glorious reward. Your past exertions will be
considered as a pledge of your future assiduity in
the faithful discharge of your duties.

CHARGE TO THE ROYAL ARCH CAPTAIN.

COMPANION: The well-known duties of your station require but little elucidation. Your office in the preparatory degrees corresponds with that of *Junior Deacon.* It is your province, conjointly with the Captain of the Host, to attend the examination of all visitors, and to take care that none are permitted to enter the Chapter, but such as have *traveled the rugged path* of trial, and evinced their title to our favor and friendship. You will be attentive to obey the commands of the Captain of the Host, during *the introduction of strangers among* the workmen; so that should they be permitted to pass your post, they may by him be introduced into the presence of the Grand Council.

The *White Banner,* entrusted to your care, is emblematical of that purity of heart and rectitude of conduct, which ought to actuate all those who pass the white veil of the sanctuary. I give it to you strongly in charge, never to suffer any one to pass your post, without the *signet of truth.*

I present you the badge of your office, in expectation of your performing your duties with intelligence, assiduity, and propriety.

CHARGE TO THE GRAND MASTER OF THE THIRD VEIL.

COMPANION : I present you with the *Scarlet Banner*, which is the ensign of your office, and with a sword to protect and defend the same. The rich and beautiful color of your banner is emblematical of *fervency* and *zeal;* it is the appropriate color of the Royal Arch degree ; it admonishes us, that we should be fervent in the exercise of our devotions to God, and zealous in our endeavors to promote the happiness of man.

CHARGE TO THE GRAND MASTER OF THE SECOND VEIL.

COMPANION : I invest you with the *Purple Banner*, which is the ensign of your office, and arm you with a sword, to enable you to maintain its honor.

The color of your banner is produced by a due mixture of *blue* and *scarlet ;* the former of which is the characteristic color of the *symbolic* or *first three degrees of masonry*, and the latter, that of the *Royal Arch degree*. It is an emblem of *union*, and is the characteristic color of the intermediate degrees. It admonishes us to cultivate and improve that spirit of union and harmony, between the brethren of the symbolic degrees and the Companions of the sublime degrees, which should ever distinguish the members of a society founded upon the principles of everlasting truth and universal philanthropy.

CHARGE TO THE GRAND MASTER OF THE FIRST VEIL.

COMPANION : I invest you with the *Blue Banner*, which is the ensign of your office, and a sword for its defence and protection. The color of your banner is one of the most durable and beautiful in nature. It is the appropriate color adopted and worn by our ancient brethren of the three symbolic degrees, and is the *peculiar characteristic* of an institution which has stood the test of ages, and which is as much distinguished by the durability of its materials or principles, as by the beauty of its superstructure. It is an emblem of universal *friendship* and *benevolence ;* and instructs us, that in the mind of a mason, those virtues should be as expansive as the blue arch of heaven itself.

CHARGE TO THE TREASURER.

COMPANION: You are elected Treasurer of this Chapter, and I have the pleasure of investing you with the badge of your office. The qualities which should recommend a Treasurer, are *accuracy* and *fidelity ;* accuracy, in keeping a fair and minute account of all receipts and disburse-

10*

ments ; fidelity, in carefully preserving all the property and funds of the Chapter, that may be placed in his hands, and rendering a just account of the same, whenever he is called upon for that purpose. I presume that your respect for the institution, your attachment to the interests of your Chapter, and your regard for a good name, which is better than precious ointment, will prompt you to the faithful discharge of the duties of your office.

CHARGE TO THE SECRETARY.

COMPANION : I with pleasure invest you with your badge as Secretary of this Chapter. The qualities which should recommend a Secretary, are, *promptitude* in issuing the notifications and orders of his superior officers; *punctuality* in attending the convocations of the Chapter ; *correctness* in recording their proceedings; *judgment* in discriminating between what is proper and what is improper to be committed to writing ; *regularity* in making his annual returns to the Grand Chapter ; *integrity* in accounting for all monies that may pass through his hands ; and *fidelity* in paying the same over into the hands of the Treasurer. The possession of these good qualities, I presume, has designated you as a suitable candidate for this important office; and I cannot entertain a doubt that you will discharge its duties beneficially to the Chapter, and honorably to yourself. And when you shall have completed the record of your transactions here below, and finished the term of your probation, may you be admitted into the celestial Grand Chapter of saints and angels, and find your name *recorded* in the *book of life eternal.*

CHARGE TO THE SENTINEL.

COMPANION: You are appointed Sentinel of this Chapter, and I invest you with the badge, and this implement of your office. As the sword is placed in the hands of the Sentinel, to enable him effectually to guard against the approach of all *cowans and eavesdroppers*, and suffer none to pass or repass but such as are *duly qualified ;* so it should morally serve as a constant admonition to us to set a guard at the entrance of our thoughts; to place a watch at the door of our lips ; to post a sentinel at the avenue of our actions ; thereby excluding every unqualified and unworthy thought, word, and deed ; and preserving consciences void of offence towards God and towards man.

As the first application from visitors for admission into the Chapter is generally made to the Sentinel at the door, your station will often present you to the observation of strangers ; it is, therefore, essentially necessary that he who sustains the office with which you are entrusted, should be a man of good morals, steady habits, strict discipline, temperate, affable and discreet. I trust that a just regard for the honor and reputation of the institution, will ever induce you to perform with fidelity the trust reposed in you ; and when the door of this earthly tabernacle shall be closed, may you find an abundant entrance through the gates into the temple and city of our God.

The Grand High Priest then delivers the following

CHARGE TO THE CHAPTER.

COMPANIONS : The exercise and management of the sublime degrees of masonry in your Chapter hitherto, are so highly appreciated, and the good reputation of the Chapter so well established, that I must presume these considerations alone, were there no others of greater magnitude, would be sufficient to induce you to preserve and perpetuate this valuable and honorable character. But when to these is added the pleasure which every philanthropic heart must feel in doing good, in promoting good order, in diffusing light and knowledge, in cultivating masonic and Christian charity, which are the great objects of this sublime institution, I cannot doubt that your future conduct, and that of your successors, will be calculated still to increase the lustre of your justly esteemed reputation.

May your *chapter* become *beautiful* as the *temple,* *peaceful* as the *ark,* and *sacred* as its *most holy place.* May your oblations of *piety* and *praise* be *grateful* as the *incense,* your love *warm* as its *flame,* and your charity diffusive as its fragrance. May your hearts be *pure* as the *altar,* and your conduct *acceptable* as the *offering.* May the exercises of your *charity* be as constant as the returning wants of the distressed *widow* and helpless *orphan.* May the approbation of Heaven be your encouragement, and the testimony of a good conscience your support : may you be endowed with every good and perfect gift, while *traveling* the *rugged path* of life, and finally be *admitted within the veil* of heaven, to the full enjoyment of life eternal. So mote it be. Amen.

The Past High Priest then makes the following proclamation :

In the name of the Most Excellent Grand Chapter of the state of . . . ., I hereby proclaim the officers of . . . . Chapter, No. . . . ., to be duly installed into their respective offices, with the private Grand Honors of Royal Arch Masonry, by three times three.

The private Grand Honors are then given.

If the installation takes place in public, the expression will be " with the public Grand Honors of Masonry by three times three," and the public Grand Honors will be given.

If the installation has taken place at the convocation immediately preceding the festival of St. John the Evangelist, the new officers will now resign their seats to the old officers, who continue to act until that day.   But if it occurs on that festival, they will retain their seats, and at once enter on the discharge of their duties for the ensuing year

SECTION III.

CEREMONIES OBSERVED AT GRAND VISITATIONS.

WHENEVER the Grand or Deputy Grand High Priest intends to visit a Chapter officially, for the purpose of inspecting its condition, the Grand Secretary should notify the High Priest of the intended visit.

The Chapter is opened in the Royal Arch degree.

The visiting officer being announced, he is received by the Chapter standing, and enters accompanied by his Grand officers, in the following order:

Grand Captain of the Host.
Grand Royal Arch Captain.
Grand Secretary, Grand Treasurer.
Grand Chaplain.
Grand Scribe, Grand King.
Grand or Deputy Grand High Priest.

The Grand Sentinel remains at the door.

They pass through the Veils, being saluted by the Masters of the Veils as they pass; and on arriving at the East, they open to the right and left, and the Grand or Deputy Grand High Priest, accompanied by the Grand King and Scribe, passes through to the Sanctum Sanctorum. The Grand Council receive them according to ancient usage, and the High Priest resigns his gavel and the chairs to the Grand High Priest and his Council. The private Grand Honors are then given, and the officers of the Chapter resign their seats to the corresponding Grand officers, the Principal Sojourner and Masters of the Veils retaining theirs.* The High Priest

* Unless the Grand Chapter is provided with the corresponding officers.

then delivers to the Grand or Deputy Grand High Priest, the Warrant of Constitution, the Treasurer's and Secretary's books, and a statement of the funds of the Chapter for his inspection. Having examined them, he makes such observations as the circumstances and situation of the Chapter may require. The Grand or Deputy Grand High Priest then resigns the chair to the High Priest, and the Grand officers leave their seats, which are reassumed by the officers of the Chapter, and repair to the East.

Should the Grand officers retire before the Chapter is closed, the same ceremony must be observed as at their entrance.

On ordinary visitations of any of the Grand officers to a subordinate Chapter, they shall be received as follows:

The Grand High Priest shall be received by the Captain of the Host and Royal Arch Captain at the door, the Chapter standing, and conducted to a seat on the right of the Grand Council, the High Priest offering him the gavel.

The Deputy Grand High Priest shall be received in the same manner, and conducted to a seat on the left of the Grand Council, the High Priest offering him the gavel.

The Grand King and Grand Scribe shall be received at the door by the Royal Arch Captain, and conducted to seats, the Grand King on the right, and the Grand Scribe on the left of the Grand Council, but the High Priest shall not offer them the gavel

The Grand Treasurer, Grand Secretary and Grand Chaplain shall be received by the Royal Arch Captain, at the White Veil, the Chapter standing, and conducted to seats, the Grand Treasurer on the right, and the Grand Secretary and Grand Chaplain on the left of the Grand Council.

These honors shall not be paid to the Grand officers unless they cause themselves to be officially announced as such at the door of the Chapter by the Sentinel.

SECTION IV.

FORM OF PROCESSION

OF A SUBORDINATE CHAPTER.

Sentinel, with flaming sword.
Mark Masters, by twos.
Past Masters, by twos.
Most Excellent Masters, by twos.
Banner of the Chapter.
Royal Arch Masons, by threes, triangularly.

*   *

*

Masters of the First and Second Veils, with their banners.
Master of the Third Veil, with his banner.
Royal Arch Captain, with his banner, and Principal
Sojourner, with his staff.
Ark of the Covenant, carried by four Companions.
Secretary and Treasurer.
Chaplain and Orator.
Scribe and King.
High Priest.

The Captain of the Host acts as Marshal, and walks at the side of the procession.

If any Grand officers are present, they will take their stations in front of the High Priest.

Processions of the Grand Chapter must be formed in the same manner, the Grand Masters of the Veils and Grand Principal Sojourner being appointed by the Grand High Priest for the occasion.

INSTALLATION OF THE OFFICERS OF A GRAND CHAPTER. *

At the time appointed for the Installation, the Grand Chapter being opened in the Royal Arch degree, the chair must be taken by some Grand or Deputy Grand High Priest, or, if none be present, by some Past Grand officer who is, or has been, a High Priest.

The highest Grand or Past Grand officer present then introduces the Grand High Priest elect, divested of all the jewels and robes of his office, to the Installing officer, saying:

Most Excellent: I hereby present before you Companion . . . ., who having been duly elected Grand High Priest of the Royal Arch Masons of . . . ., now declares himself ready for installation.

The Grand High Priest elect then turning and facing the Companions, the Installing officer says:

Companions: You now behold before you Companion . . . ., who has been duly elected to preside over you as your Grand High Priest, and who now declares himself ready for installation.

---

* This service, prepared by the Author of the present work, was adopted by the General Grand Chapter of the United States, at its session in 1856 at Hartford.

If any of you have any reasons to urge why he should not be installed, you will make your objections known now, or else forever hereafter hold your peace.

If no objections are made, he will continue to say:

Hearing no objections, I shall proceed to install him.

The Installing officer then administers the following obligation of office—all the Companions standing:

I, ... , do promise and swear that I will serve as Grand High Priest of the Royal Arch Masons of . . . . , for the term for which I have been elected, and will perform all the duties of that office to the best of my abilities, and will support and maintain the Constitution of the Grand Chapter of . . . . , *and that of the General Grand Chapter of the United States.* So help me God.

The Grand Chaplain shall then offer the following

PRAYER.

Most holy and glorious Lord **God**, the Great High Priest of Heaven and Earth; we approach thee with reverence, and implore thy blessing on the Companion appointed to preside over our ancient fraternity;—fill his heart with thy fear, that his tongue and actions may pronounce thy will;—make him steadfast in thy service; grant him firmness of mind and kindness of disposition ; teach him to rule his brethren, not with a rod of iron, but with justice and equity ; animate his heart and strengthen his endeavors to do good. May he inculcate thy judgments and thy laws, and do all that his high office requires, with an eye single to thy glory and the good of the craft! Bless him, and bless those thou hast put under him ; and grant that when we shall have finished the work of this earthly temple of our bodies, we may be admitted to the glories of that second temple of the spirit, eternal in the heavens.

Glory be to God on high.

Response, by all the Companions:

Response. As it was in the beginning, is now, and ever shall be, world without end. Amen. So mote it be.

The Installing officer will then invest the Grand High Priest elect, with the robes and jewels of his office, after which he will deliver to him the following

CHARGE :

Most Excellent: By the voice of your Companions you have been chosen to occupy the most important and the most honorable office in their power to bestow ; and to me has been intrusted the pleasing duty of investing you with its insignia.

You have been too long a member of our ancient

and honorable craft, to require now any instructions in relation to the duties of your office ; and I do not doubt that you will be constant and regular in your attendance on the convocations of the Grand Chapter ; watching with fidelity and diligence the conduct of the subordinate bodies within your jurisdiction ; paying punctual attention to the constitution of our order, and requiring a due obedience to it from every member ; and in all things, making the glory of the Grand High Priest of the universe, and the good of the Craft, the chief objects of your regard.

The ancient landmarks of the order, by which we are distinguished from the rest of the world, are peculiarly intrusted to your care ; and it therefore becomes your most sacred duty to see that, during your administration, not the least of them may be removed.

From our knowledge of your zeal and ability, we feel confident that you will discharge the duties of this important station in such a manner as will greatly redound to the honor of yourself, as well as of the fraternity over whom you have been elected to preside.

Let the *Mitre* with which you are invested, remind you of the dignity of the office you sustain, and its inscription impress upon your mind a sense of your dependence upon God ;—that perfection is not given unto man upon earth, and that perfect holiness belongeth alone unto the Lord.

The *Breast-Plate*, with which you are decorated, in imitation of that upon which were engraven the names of the twelve tribes, and worn by the High Priest of Israel, is to teach you that you are always to bear in mind your responsibility to the laws and ordinances of the institution, and that the honor and interests of our order and its members, should be always near your heart.

The *various colors* of the *Robes* you wear, are emblematical of every grace and virtue which can adorn and beautify the human mind, whose cultivation and constant practice are as necessary to your own present and future happiness, as they are, by the example they will afford, to the prosperity of the craft over whom you are placed.

You will now assume your seat in the East, and instruct your subordinates in the duties which they are respectively required to discharge.

After he has taken his seat in the East, the Grand Captain of the Host will say:

Companions, in the name of **the Most High God**, I do hereby proclaim Companion . . . . , Most Excellent Grand High Priest of the Royal Arch Masons of . . . . , with the grand honors of masonry by three times three.

The grand honors of Royal Arch Masonry are then given. The Deputy Grand High Priest is then presented to the Grand High Priest in the same way, and after taking a similar obligation, the Grand High Priest delivers the following

CHARGE TO THE MOST EXCELLENT DEP. GR. HIGH PRIEST.

MOST EXCELLENT: The station to which you have been called by your Companions, is one of great dignity and importance. In many cases, your powers and prerogatives are coextensive with those of your chief; and at all times you are, if he be present, to assist him with your counsel and co-operation, and, in his absence, to preside over the craft. But while your powers and privileges are thus extensive, remember that they bring with them a heavy share of responsibility. The honor that has been conferred upon you, and the trust that has been reposed in you, demand a corresponding fidelity and attachment to the interests of those to whose kindness and confidence you are indebted for your official elevation.

The signification of the robes you wear, you have already heard explained. May the symbolic lessons which they convey be deeply impressed upon your mind and heart, and ever influence your conduct.

The Grand King is then presented, in the following words:

MOST EXCELLENT: I here present before you Companion . . . ., who has been duly elected to serve this Grand Chapter as Grand King, and who now declares himself ready for installation.

The Grand King elect then turning and facing the Companions, the Grand High Priest says:

COMPANIONS: You now behold before you Companion ...., who has been duly elected to serve this Grand Chapter as Right Excellent Grand King, and who now declares himself ready for installation. If any of you have any reasons to urge why he should not be installed, you will make them known now, or else forever hereafter hold your peace.

If no objections are made, he will say:

Hearing no objections, I shall proceed to install him.

The Grand High Priest will then administer the following obligation:

I, ..., do promise and swear that I will serve this Grand Chapter, as Right Excellent Grand King, for the time for which I have been elected; that I will perform all the duties appertaining to that office to the best of my abilities, and will support and maintain the Constitution of the Grand Chapter of ...., *and that of the General Grand Chapter of the United States.* So help me God.

The Grand High Priest will then cause the Grand King to be invested with the robes and jewels of his office, and deliver to him the following

CHARGE TO THE RIGHT EXCELLENT GRAND KING.

RIGHT EXCELLENT COMPANION: The important station to which you have been elected requires from you exemplary conduct; and its duties demand your most assiduous attention. In the absence of the Grand High Priest and his Deputy, you are to preside; in their presence, you are to strengthen and support the authority of your chief, and to aid him by your counsel and advice.

The *Scarlet Robe*, an emblem of royal dignity, should remind you of the paternal concern you should ever feel for our institution, and the fervency and zeal with which you should endeavor to promote its prosperity.

In presenting to you the *Crown*, which is an emblem of royalty, I would remind you, that to reign sovereign in the hearts and affections of men, must be far more grateful to a generous and benevolent mind than to rule over their lives and fortunes; and that to enable you to enjoy this pre-eminence with honor and satisfaction, you must subject your own passions and prejudices to the dominion of reason and charity.

The remaining officers are introduced and obligated in the same way, after which each receives his special charge as follows:

CHARGE TO THE RIGHT EXCELLENT GRAND SCRIBE.

RIGHT EXCELLENT COMPANION: The office of Grand Scribe, to which you are elected, is very important

11

and respectable. In the absence of your superior officers, you are bound to succeed them, and to perform their duties. The purposes of the institution ought never to suffer for want of intelligence in its proper officers ; you will therefore perceive the necessity there is of your possessing such qualifications as will enable you to accomplish those duties which are incumbent upon you, in your appropriate station, as well as those which may occasionally devolve on you, by the absence of your superiors.

The *Purple Robe*, with which you are invested, is an emblem of *union*, and is calculated to remind you that the harmony and unanimity of the order should be your constant aim ; and to this end you are studiously to avoid all occasions of giving offence, or countenancing anything that may create divisions or dissensions. You are, by all means in your power, to endeavor to establish a permanent union and good understanding among all orders and degrees of masonry ; and as the glorious sun, at its meridian height, dispels the mist and clouds which obscure the horizon, so may your exertions tend to dissipate the gloom of jealousy and discord, whenever they may appear.

CHARGE TO THE RIGHT EXCELLENT GRAND TREASURER.

RIGHT EXCELLENT COMPANION : You have been elected to the responsible office of Grand Treasurer, and I now invest you with the badge of your office.

It is your duty to receive all moneys due the Grand Chapter, from the hands of the Grand Secretary; make due entries of the same, and pay them out by order of the Grand High Priest, and with the consent and approbation of the Grand Chapter. The office to which you have been elected, embraces an important trust, and the choice of you by your companions is an evidence of the high opinion they entertain of your fidelity and discretion.

CHARGE TO THE RIGHT EXCELLENT GRAND SECRETARY.

RIGHT EXCELLENT COMPANION : You have been elected to the important office of Grand Secretary, and I now invest you with the jewel of your office.

It is your duty to receive all moneys due the Grand Chapter, and pay them over to the Grand Treasurer, taking his receipt for the same ; to observe all the proceedings of the Grand Chapter, and to make a true record of all things proper to be written. You are also the official organ of the Grand Chapter, and in that capacity will conduct its various correspondence, and act as the medium of intercourse between the fraternity and their presiding officer. In the discharge of these extensive duties, let your carriage and behavior be marked with that promptitude and discretion that will at once reflect credit on yourself, and honor on the body whom you represent.

CHARGE TO THE RIGHT REVEREND GRAND CHAPLAIN.

RIGHT REVEREND COMPANION: The sacred position of Grand Chaplain has been intrusted to your care, and I now invest you with the jewel of your office.

In the discharge of your duties, you will be required to conduct the devotional exercises of our grand convocations, and to perform the sacred functions of your holy calling at our public seminaries. Though masonry be not religion, it is emphatically religion's handmaid; and I am sure that, in ministering at its altar, the services you may perform will lose nothing of their vital importance, because they are practised in that spirit of universal tolerance which distinguishes our institution. The doctrines of morality and virtue which you are accustomed to inculcate to the world, as the minister of God, will form the appropriate lessons which you are expected to communicate to your Companions. The profession which you have chosen as your lot in life, is the best guaranty that you will discharge the duties of your present appointment with steadfastness and perseverance in well-doing.

CHARGE TO THE EXCELLENT GR. CAPTAIN OF THE HOST.

EXCELLENT COMPANION: The office with which you have been intrusted is of great importance, and requires much skill and attention for the faithful discharge of its duties, which are those of a marshal, or master of ceremonies.

You are to superintend all processions of the Grand Chapter, when moving as a distinct body, either in public or private; and as the world can only judge of our private discipline by our public deportment, you will be careful that the utmost order and decorum be observed on all such occasions. You will ever be attentive to the commands of your chief, and always near at hand to see them duly executed. I invest you with the badge of your office, and presume that you will give to your duties all that study and attention which their importance demands. I present you with this sword, as the appropriate implement of your office.

CHARGE TO THE EXCELLENT GRAND PRINCIPAL SOJOURNER.

EXCELLENT COMPANION: The office confided to you is one of great importance, though subordinate in degree. Occupying a station which corresponds to that of Senior Deacon in the lower degrees, it becomes your duty to obey and extend the orders of your superiors, and to act as their proxies in the active business of the Grand Chapter. Attention, obedience, and promptitude are, therefore, essentially necessary for the faithful performance of your duties. I present you with the rod, a symbol of command, as the proper ensign of your office.

CHARGE TO THE EXCELLENT GRAND ROYAL ARCH CAPTAIN.

EXCELLENT COMPANION : The office to which you have been elected nearly corresponds to that of Junior Deacon in the inferior degrees. It is, therefore, your duty to see that the external avenues of the Grand Chapter are securely guarded, and that none are permitted to pass or repass, but such as are duly qualified, and have the requisite permission. Let vigilance and attention, therefore, actuate you in the discharge of the functions of your important office ; for the more faithful performance of which, I intrust this sword to your keeping.

CHARGE TO THE GRAND SENTINEL.

COMPANION : You have been appointed Grand Sentinel of this Grand Chapter, and I now invest you with the jewel of your office, and place this sword in your hands, the more effectually to enable you to repel the approach of cowans and eavesdroppers, and to guard against surprise.

It is your duty to guard the door of the Grand Chapter, on the outside; to report to the Grand Royal Arch Captain those who desire to be admitted ; to place the Chapter room in order for convocations ; and to attend to such other duties as may be required of you by the Grand Chapter. Your punctual attendance is essentially necessary at every convocation.

The Grand Captain of the Host then makes proclamation as follows:

By authority of the Most Excellent Grand Chapter of ......, I proclaim that the Grand officers have been installed in ample form, with the grand honors of masonry, by three times three.

The public or private grand honors of masonry, accordingly as the installation shall have been publicly or privately conducted, shall then be given, and the installation ceremony will be concluded.

On public occasions these ceremonies may be preceded and followed by anthems, odes, and addresses, at the discretion of the Grand Chapter.

SECTION VI.

CONSTITUTIONAL RULES

FOUNDED ON THE

ANCIENT LANDMARKS AND USAGES OF ROYAL ARCH MASONRY.

1. WHEN the Grand High Priest is absent from the Grand Chapter, the chair shall be taken by the Deputy. If both are absent, the Grand King, or if he be likewise absent, the Grand Scribe must take the chair. If all these officers are absent, the Senior Past Grand officer present must preside. If no such Grand officer be present, the duty will devolve on the High Priest of the oldest Chapter present.

2. When the High Priest of a Chapter is absent, his duties must be performed by the King and Scribe in succession. If they should likewise be absent, the chair must be taken by a Past High Priest of the Chapter; but if no such Past High Priest be present, the Chapter cannot be opened. The Warrant of Constitution is granted to the High Priest, King, and Scribe, and their successors in office, and to none else; and none else can lawfully act.

3. No officer of the Grand or a Subordinate Chapter, can be recognized as such until he has been installed.

4. Every officer shall hold on to his office until his successor has been installed.

5. No officer can resign his office after he has been installed. Nor can any election be held, except at the constitutional convocation for that purpose, unless by dispensation.

6. No Chapter can, at an extra convocation, alter or expunge the proceedings of a regular one.

7. No Chapter can interfere in the business of another Chapter, or give degrees to candidates who have been accepted by other Chapters, without their consent.

8. No resident of any state in which there is a Chapter, can receive the degrees in any Chapter in another state, unless with the approbation of the Chapter nearest his place of residence.

9. The degrees of Mark, Past, and Most Excellent Master, and Royal Arch, are the only degrees which can be conferred in a Chapter.

10. No candidate can be permitted to receive the Chapter degrees who is deformed, maimed, or imperfect in his limbs, or whose physical defects are such as to prevent him from conforming literally to all the requirements of the several degrees.

11. No candidate can be elected to receive the degrees, nor any Royal Arch Mason admitted a member of any Chapter, except by a unanimous vote in his favor.

12. All ballotings for candidates, and trials of Companions, must take place in the Royal Arch degree. But a brother who is not a Royal Arch Mason, may be tried in the degree to which he has attained.

13. None but Royal Arch Masons can be permitted to make any motion, vote, or join in any debate.

14. Every Subordinate Chapter, as well as every member of the same, has the right of appeal to the Grand Chapter, whose decision shall be final.

15. There can be no appeal to the General Grand Chapter from the decisions of a Grand Chapter.

16. Every Chapter must meet at least once in three months, and no Chapter can suspend its convocations, unless by dispensation from the Grand Chapter, or Presiding Grand officer.

11*

17. No Chapter can be opened unless there be nine Royal Arch Masons present.

18. No Chapter can be opened, or held, except by the authority of a warrant from the Grand Chapter, or a dispensation from the Grand or Deputy Grand High Priest.

19. Neither more nor less than three candidates can be exalted at one and the same time.

20. It is not necessary for the due and legal discharge of his functions, that a High Priest should receive the degree of High **Priesthood.** **But it is recommended** that every High Priest should, as soon as convenient after his election, apply to a convention of High Priests for admission into that order.

21. No Chapter in one state can work under a warrant granted by the Grand Chapter of another state.

22. No *ex post facto* law can be made in the Grand Chapter, or any Subordinate Chapter.

23. No warrant or dispensation can be granted for the opening of a new Chapter, except upon the petition of nine regular Royal Arch Masons.

24. The election of officers in Subordinate Chapters must be held at the stated convocation next preceding the festival of St. John the Evangelist, and the installation must take place as soon after the election as possible. Where from any cause the election has not been held at the stated period, a dispensation from the Grand or Deputy Grand High Priest will be required, for holding it at any subsequent time.

25. No Chapter can suspend its by-laws.

26. There can be no appeal from the decision of the Presiding officer of a Chapter, to the Chapter. The Grand Chapter, alone, can reverse such decision.

27. Every Chapter must consist of the following officers: High Priest, King, Scribe, Captain of the Host, Principal Sojourner, Royal Arch Captain, Masters of the Third, Second and **First Veils,** Treasurer, Secretary, and **Sentinel.**

APPENDIX.

Forms of Masonic Documents.

" As these formal and orderly parts are calculated to convey the meaning in the clearest, distinctest and most effectual manner, and have been well considered and settled by the wisdom of successive ages, it is prudent not to depart from them without good reason or urgent necessity."

BLACKSTONE'S COMMENTARIES.

MASONIC DOCUMENTS.

I.

Form of a Petition for a Dispensation to Open and Hold a New Chapter.

To the Most Excellent Grand High Priest of the Grand Chapter of the State of ...... :

[Date.]

WE, the undersigned, being Royal Arch Masons in good standing, and having the prosperity of the Royal Craft at heart, are anxious to exert our best endeavors to promote and diffuse the genuine principles of Royal Arch Masonry, and for the convenience of our respective dwellings, and other good reasons, us thereunto moving, we are desirous of forming a new Chapter at ......, in the ...... of ......, to be named ...... Chapter.

We, therefore, pray for a Dispensation empowering us to open and hold a regular Chapter at ...... aforesaid, and therein to discharge the duties and enjoy the privileges of Royal Arch Masonry, according to the landmarks and usages of the order, and the constitution and laws of the Grand Chapter.

And we do hereby nominate and recommend Companion A.... B.... to be our first Most Excellent High Priest; Companion C.... D.... to be our first King, and Companion E.... F.... to be our first Scribe.

And should the prayer of this petition be granted, we do hereby promise a strict conformity to the constitution, laws and edicts of the Grand Chapter of the State of ......, *and to the constitution of the General Grand Chapter of the United States,** so far as they may come to our knowledge.

[This Dispensation must be signed by not less than *nine* Royal Arch Masons.]

It may be presented to either the **Grand** or Deputy Grand High Priest, and must be accompanied with the recommendation of the nearest Chapter working under a warrant of constitution, which recommendation should be in the following words:

* These words in italics may be omitted in those states whose Grand Chapters are not in union with the General Grand Chapter.

II.

Form of Recommendation.

To the Most Excellent Grand High Priest of the Grand Chapter of ....:

At a .... convocation of ...... Chapter .... No. ...., holden at ....,
on the .... day of ......, A∴ L∴ 585, A∴ I∴ 238—

The petition of several Companions, praying for a Dispensation to open a
new Chapter at ......, in the ...... of ......, was duly laid before the
Chapter, when it was

Resolved, **That this Chapter,** being fully satisfied that the petitioners are
Royal Arch Masons, in good standing, and being prepared to vouch for their
moral character and masonic abilities, does, therefore, recommend that the
Dispensation prayed for be granted to them.

A true **copy** of the records.

............., *Secretary.*

Upon the receipt of this petition, with the accompanying recommendation,
the Grand or Deputy Grand High Priest is authorized to issue his Dispensation, under his private seal, for opening and holding the new Chapter, which
Dispensation should be in the following words:

III.

Form of Dispensation for Opening and Holding a New Chapter.

To all whom it may concern:

KNOW YE, That I, ..., Most Excellent Grand High Priest of
the Grand Chapter of the State of ......, have received a petition from a
constitutional number of Companions, who have been properly vouched for
and recommended, which petition sets forth that they are desirous of forming
a new Chapter at ......, in the ...... of ......; and, whereas, there
appears to me to be good and sufficient cause for granting the prayer of the
said petition:

Now, therefore, by virtue of the powers in me vested by the constitutions
of the order, I do hereby grant this my Dispensation, authorizing and empowering **Companion** A.... B.... to act as Most Excellent High Priest;
Companion **C.... D....** to act as King, and Companion E.... F.... to
act as Scribe, of a Chapter to be holden at ......, in the ...... of ... ...
to be named and designated as ...... Chapter.

And I do hereby further authorize and empower the said Companions,
with the necessary assistance, to open and hold Lodges of Mark, Past and
Most Excellent Masters, and a Chapter of Royal Arch Masons, and therein
to Advance, Induct, Receive and Acknowledge candidates in the several
preparatory degrees, and to Exalt the same to the Holy Royal Arch, according to the ancient landmarks and usages of the order, and the constitution;

of the Grand Chapter of the State of ...., *and of the General Grand Chapter of the United States,** but not otherwise.

And this Dispensation shall remain of force until the Grand Chapter aforesaid shall grant a Warrant of Constitution for the said Chapter, or until it shall be revoked by me, or by the authority of the Grand Chapter.

<pre>
 *****   Given under my hand and seal, at ......, this
 * Seal *   .... day of ......, A. L. 535.., A. I. 238...
 ******   .... *Grand High Priest.*
</pre>

At the next convocation of the Grand Chapter this Dispensation is returned, and the Grand Chapter will, if there be no just reason to the contrary, grant a Warrant of Constitution, which shall be in the following language:

IV.

Form of a Warrant of Constitution.

To all whom it may concern:

The Most Excellent Grand Royal Arch Chapter of ......, assembled in Grand Convocation in the city of ......, and state aforesaid,

Send Greeting:

KNOW YE, That we, the Grand Royal Arch Chapter of ......, do hereby authorize and empower our trusty and well-beloved Companions, A.... B...., High Priest; C.... D...., King; and E.... F...., Scribe, to open and hold a Royal Arch Chapter at ......, in the...... of ......, to be known and designated on our register as ...... Chapter, No. .., and therein to exalt candidates to the august degree of the Holy Royal Arch, according to the ancient landmarks and usages of Royal Arch Masonry, and not otherwise.

And we do further authorize and empower our said trusty and well-beloved Companions, A.... B...., C.... D...., and E.... F...., to open and hold, under the jurisdiction of the said Chapter, Lodges, and confer the degrees of Mark, Past, and Most Excellent Master, and therein to Advance, Induct, Receive and Acknowledge candidates, according to the aforesaid landmarks and usages of the craft, and not otherwise.

And we do further authorize and empower our said trusty and well-beloved Companions, A.... B...., C.... D...., and E.... F...., to install their successors, duly elected and chosen, to invest them with all the powers and dignities to their offices respectively belonging, and to deliver to them this Warrant of Constitution; and such successors shall, in like manner, from time to time, install their successors, and proceed in the premises as above

---

* These words in italics to be omitted in states not under the jurisdiction of the General Grand Chapter.

directed—such installation to be on or before the festival of St. John the Evangelist.

Provided always, that the above-named Companions and their successors do pay and cause to be paid, due respect and obedience to the Most Excellent Grand Royal Chapter of ...... aforesaid, and to the edicts, rules and regulations thereof; otherwise, this Warrant of Constitution to be of no force nor virtue.

> Given in Grand Convocation, under the hands of our
> Grand officers, and the Seal of our Grand Chap-
> ter, at ......, this ...... day of ......, in the
> year of light 585.., and of the discovery 238...

G.... H....,   L.... M...., *Grand King.*
  Grand High Priest. ***** N.... O...., *Grand Scribe.*
J.... K....,   * Seal. *
  Deputy G. H. Priest. *****
  R.... S...., *Grand Secretary.*

When a warrant is granted to a new Chapter, which is at so great a distance as to render it inconvenient for the Grand officers to personally attend the constitution of the Chapter and the installation of the officers, the Grand High Priest may issue the following instrument, **under his** hand and private seal, directed to some Past High Priest:

V

Certificate of Proxy, Authorizing a Past High Priest to Constitute a New Chapter, and to Install Its Officers.

To all whom it may concern:

But more especially to Companions A.... B...., Most Excellent High Priest elect; C.... D...., King elect; E... F...., Scribe elect, and the other Companions who have been empowered by a Warrant of Constitution issued under the authority of the Most Excellent Grand Chapter of ......, to assemble as a regular Chapter at ......, in the ...... of ......, and to be known and designated as ..... Chapter, No. ...

KNOW YE, That, reposing all trust and confidence in the skill, prudence and integrity of our Most Excellent Companion ...., I have thought proper—being myself unable to attend—to nominate and appoint the said Most Excellent Companion .... to constitute, *in form*, the Companions aforesaid into a regular Chapter, and to install the officers elect, according to the ancient usages of the craft, and for so doing this shall be his sufficient warrant.

*****
* Seal. *   Given under my hand and seal, at ......, this
*****   .... day of ......, in the year of light 585..,
     and of the discovery 238...

            G.... H...., *Grand High Priest.*

VI.

m of Petition for the Capitular Degrees

[Date.]

To the Most Excellent High Priest, King, Scribe and Companions of ..... *Chapter, No.* ....:

The undersigned, a Master Mason, and member of ...... Lodge, No. .., under the jurisdiction of the Grand Lodge of ......, having the good of the craft at heart, and being desirous of obtaining further light in Masonry, fraternally offers himself as a candidate for the degrees conferred in your Chapter. Should his petition be granted, he promises a cheerful compliance with all the forms and usages of the fraternity. His residence is in ......, and his occupation that of a ......

[Signed] A.... B.....

[To be recommended by two Royal Arch Masons.]

VII.

Form of a Petition for Membership.

[Date.]

To the Most Excellent High Priest, King, Scribe and Companions of .... *Chapter, No.* ...:

COMPANIONS:

The undersigned, a Royal Arch Mason, formerly a member of ...... Chapter, No. .., at ......, under the jurisdiction of the Grand Chapter of ......, fraternally prays to be admitted as a member of your Chapter.

[Signed] B.... C.....

[To be recommended by two Royal Arch Masons.]

VIII.

Form of a Demit from a Chapter.

To all Royal Arch Masons to whom these presents shall come, Greeting:

This is to certify that Companion ...... is, at the date of these presents, a Royal Arch Mason, in good and regular standing; and that, having paid all dues, and being free from all charges, he is, at his own request, by the vote of the Chapter, dismissed from membership in ...... Chapter, No. ..., under the jurisdiction of the Grand Chapter of ......

Seal of the Chapter.

Given under my hand and the seal of the Chapter, at ...., this .... day of ...., in the year of light 585.., and of the discovery 238...

...., *Secretary.*

IX.

Form of a Royal Arch Diploma.

HOLINESS TO THE LORD.

To all Enlightened, Advanced, Pass-
ed, Received and Acknowledged
and Exalted Masons throughout
the world:
　　　Thrice Greeting:

WE, the Officers of the Grand Royal
Arch Chapter of ......, do hereby
certify that the bearer, our well-beloved Companion ......, who hath,
in the margin hereof, signed his name,
has been regularly admitted to the
degrees of Mark, Past and Most Excellent Master, and exalted to the
august degree of the Holy Royal Arch,
having sustained with fortitude the
severe trials of skill and constancy
required from all previous to their admission into this sublime Order. And
as such, we recommend him to all our
excellent and well-beloved Companions throughout the two hemispheres.
Given under our hands and the seal
　of the Grand Chapter, at ......,
　this .... day of ......, in the year
　of light 585.., and of the discovery
　238...

SANCTUM DOMINO.

Omnibus Architectonibus, Illumi-
natis, Promotis, Expertis, Re-
ceptis et Recognitis atque Excelsis
per Orbem Terrarum:
　　　S∴ S∴ S∴

Nos, Præfecti Summi Capituli Arcus
Regalis [name of the state] testamur
et certum facimus socium nostrum
dilectissimum .... qui hujusce
in margine, nomen suum ascripsit,
post debitas constitutasque scientiæ
et constantiæ probationes, gradibus
Magistri Insigniti, Experti et Excel-
lentissimi cumulatum esse, et in ordi-
nem augustum Architectonum Arcus
Sancti Regalis rite evectum. Eum
igitur cum singulis juribus ad istos
gradus pertinentibus, omnibus sociis
commendamus.

In cujus rei testimonium manus
nostras et sigillum Summi Capituli his presentibus apponi
curavimus .... hac die
.... mensis .... Anno Lucis
585.., et post inventionem
238∴..

Ne varietur.

.... *Grand High Priest.*

.... *Grand King.*

```
***********
*   Seal   *
*  of the  *
* G. Chapter. *
***********
```

.... *Deputy G. High Priest.*

.... *Grand Scribe.*

.... *Grand Secretary.*

[When the High Priest, King or Scribe of a Chapter cannot in person attend the convocation of the Grand Chapter, it is competent for him to grant a proxy to some member of his Chapter, duly qualified to represent him in the Grand Chapter. and he must then furnish him with the following certificate :

X

Form of a Certificate for a Proxy in the Grand Chapter

To the Grand Chapter of . . . .

This is to certify that I have hereby appointed Companion . . . . my proxy, to represent me as . . . . . . of . . . . . . Chapter, No. . ., in the convocation of the Grand Chapter of . . . . . .,to be holden at . . . . . ., on the . . . . day of . . . . . ., 185 . . .

Witness my hand and seal, at . . . . . .,

this . . . . day of . . . . . ., 185 . . .

. . . ., *of* . . . . . . *Chapter, No.* . . .

XI.

Date of Royal Arch Documents.

Each of the systems of Masonry has a date peculiar to itself, and which, as referring to some important event in its history, is affixed to its official documents. Thus the epoch of the creation of light in the beginning of the world, according to the Mosaic cosmogony, has been assumed, for a symbolical reason, as the era of Ancient Craft Masonry, and hence all documents connected with the first three degrees are dated from this period, which date is found by adding 4000 to the vulgar era, and is called in the year of light, or *Anno Lucis,* usually abbreviated A∴ L∴—thus the present year, 1858, in a masonic document of the symbolic degrees, would be designated as A∴ L∴ 5858.

Royal Arch Masons use this date also, but in addition to it they commence their peculiar era with the year in which the building of the second temple was begun, at which time their traditions inform them that a discovery important to the craft was made. They call their era the year of the discovery or *Anno Inventionis,* sometimes abbreviated A∴ I∴ or *A∴ Inv∴.* The second temple was commenced 530 years before Christ, and hence the Royal Arch date is found by adding that number of years to the Christian era. Thus the present year, 1858, in a Royal Arch document, would be designated as Anno Inventionis 2388, and combining the two masonic eras, such a document would properly be designated thus: "Anno Lucis 5858, and Anno Inventionis 2388." or, "in the Year of Light 5858, and of the Discovery 2388."